DATE DUE

JUL 2 1 1994		
AUG 1 9 1994		

Printed
in USA

Individualized Instruction Through Differentiated Learning Programs

Also by the Author:

Individualized Teaching in the Elementary Schools.
Dona Stahl and Patricia Anzalone, 1970, Parker.

Individualized Instruction Through Differentiated Learning Programs

Dona K. Stahl

Parker Publishing Company, Inc.

West Nyack, New York

Library of Congress Cataloging in Publication Data

Stahl, Dona Kofod.
  Individualized instruction through differentiated
learning programs.

  Includes bibliographical references and index.
  1. Individualized instruction.   I.   Title.
LB1031.S68   372.1'39'4   75-26756
ISBN 0-13-457101-0

To My Husband

Howard

How This Book Will Help the Professional Educator

The successful teacher is one who is familiar with a wide variety of approaches to learning and has a knack for matching the "right" way with the right child at the right time. This teacher makes certain the instructional program is flexible and varied, yet organized and controlled. Much of the success of such a program is based on a realistic understanding of what the teacher should expect from children, and skill in pinpointing their uniquenesses. You can be this teacher, and you can have this kind of program.

Every chapter that follows will help you develop just such an instructional program. You will be guided step-by-step into many approaches for differentiating and individualizing instruction. Specific practical suggestions for taking your first exploratory steps into differentiated instruction will eliminate much of the fear of the unknown which often hinders teachers from expanding their horizons. Other plans and suggestions will delve into more extensive programs for individualization and provide guidelines for avoiding many of the pitfalls which await the teacher inclined to take an enthusiastic but premature plunge. You will have the comfortable assurance that it is not necessary or even desirable to give up traditional techniques in order to individualize an instructional program. The ten chapters in this book are full of practical, timely, easy-to-implement suggestions to add to your storehouse of instructional strategies and know-how.

The first part of the book stresses organizational and stage-setting aspects of a differentiated instructional program. Chapter 1 contains a practical discussion which lays the groundwork for turning theory into practice. Guidelines for employing both formal and informal diagnostic procedures are included in Chapter 2 and will give you many practical ways of finding out about your students' abilities,.

interests, strengths and weaknesses. Chapter 3 approaches the task of preliminary planning for instruction and includes helpful suggestions on how to adopt the behavioral objectives concept to an individualized program. The next two chapters deal with environmental factors and provide many ideas for conquering problems of space, time, instructional materials and the emotional/psychological atmosphere.

Once these important points have been resolved, attention turns naturally to the action which will take place in the setting which has been established. The second part of the book contains a subject-by-subject discussion of individualizing instruction. Many experiences and case studies are included that will show how teachers have actually planned a variety of approaches to differentiated learning opportunities in each subject area. Here you will find a synthesis of many concepts developed in the earlier chapters. This portion of the book illustrates practical ways of applying ideas and guidelines in your differentiated programs of instruction.

Much of the excitement and reward of education is found in the continuing search for better ways of working with children in the school setting. We are constantly on the alert to discover more about how children learn and to find new approaches to instruction which we can put into practice. Our goal is better learning opportunities for all children. In working toward this goal, it is necessary to find practical ways of implementing instructional programs which provide for differentiated learning. This, in turn, requires effective program designing by the classroom teacher and opportunities to exchange experiences and ideas.

Designing effective programs for differentiated learning; sharing experiences and practical ideas—that is what this book is all about.

Dona K. Stahl

Table of Contents

9

Establishing a Strong Basis
for Differentiated Learning
Programs

———————————————————————— 1

Once upon a time an automotive company produced 120 automobiles of various sizes, models and colors. Some were four-cylinder models, others had six cylinders and still others boasted eight cylinders in the standard V arrangement. Wheelbases, weight and horsepower varied among the automobiles. As the 120 cars were purchased and taken home, they were used for many different kinds of driving. Elderly owners drove theirs infrequently, at moderate speeds and for short distances. City dwellers, suburban housewives, teenage drivers and traveling salesmen all exposed their automobiles to different kinds of driving conditions. The more fortunate automobiles were given tender loving care with frequent washing, the best gasoline and the shelter of garages when not in use, but not all were treated with this kind of affection and consideration.

As the cars became a little older, they were taken into a local garage for attention, repair and tuning-up. Specific cars were assigned to each of four mechanics who became rather familiar with them as the year progressed. About once a year, new mechanics were assigned to take care of the automobiles. During this time, the owners continued in their established patterns of using the cars. Many of them became less particular about their automobiles: parts became worn out or rusted, oil wasn't changed as often as it should be, dents and scratches were left unattended. Each year as new mechanics were appointed to work on the cars, they found more and more to complain about.

"I can't understand why this red four-door doesn't get better gas mileage. These others seem to do so much better."

"This station wagon is certainly a slow starter, it must have been a lemon right from the beginning."

"Well, I don't know, Mr. Thomas, this car of yours is awfully sluggish. Nothing I do seems to give it any get up and go. Maybe you should try the specialist they have across the street. He may be able to give it more attention than I can."

"What I can't figure out is what have those other mechanics been doing all these years? You'd think these cars would be in better shape than they are. How does anyone expect me to do something with them when the darn things won't even turn over when you try to start them?"

"I mean, after all, they were all made the same year. You'd think they would all be capable of the same performance now."

Ridiculous? Of course. No one really expects to get the same speed, the same mileage, the same performance from such a variety of models, sizes and horsepowers. It wasn't even expected when they were new. There were too many variations among too many factors to ever make equality of performance a realistic expectation.

So, what does all this have to do with teaching? Let's just go back a bit and paraphrase what some of our hypothetical mechanics were complaining about.

"I can't understand why Mary Ann has such a short attention span. All the others can pay attention when I give instructions."

"That Johnny Burns is certainly a slow starter. He must have been born lazy."

"Well, I don't know, Mr. Thomas, this young son of yours is a very reluctant learner. Nothing I do seems to motivate him to do better. Maybe you should take him to the specialist at the learning clinic. He can give your boy the individual attention he needs."

"What I can't figure out is what have those other teachers been doing all these years. You'd think these kids would have learned more than they have. How does anyone expect me to teach them something when they can't even read?"

"I mean, after all, they are the same age and have all been through the first three grades. You'd think they would all be able to read these fourth-grade social studies books."

Ridiculous? Of course. No one really expects to have the same achievement level, the same rate of learning, the same performance from such a variety of youngsters with all their individual differences. . . .

Or *is* uniformity of achievement and ability just what we *do* expect? Take a look at the way we prepare for the new school year and a new batch of youngsters. Certain rituals are carefully observed, speeches made and parades held on the First Day of School. These phenomena reveal a great deal about what we expect from children and what we expect of education.

First Day of School speeches are among the earliest items on the agenda. Such speeches are a popular means by which teachers introduce certain conventions which prevail in the school environment. One such convention is the establishment of the *we-you* orientation: we the authority figures—you the subjects; we the imparters of knowledge and wisdom—you the intakers; we the determiners of content and direction—you the followers.

A second convention generally reinforced in First Day of School speeches is the convention of compartmentalization. This convention has been refined to the point where not only knowledge but people, space and time are categorized and rather rigidly labeled.

Here is your class, these are your classmates—you are all second graders. This is your regular teacher, Miss X is the music teacher, Mrs. Y will be the reading teacher for your group—and, if you need guidance or counseling, see Mr. Z.

This classroom is B-14. You will go to C-9 for art. For reading you will either stay here or go to A-3, A-7 or the remedial reading room. You will eat and watch assembly programs in B-2 and will go to C-1 if you are ill.

The first thing every morning we will have "opening exercises," attendance and lunch count. This will be followed by show-and-tell for ten minutes. Reading will be from 9:30 to 11:00, and if you have been very good we will have recess for 15 minutes before we start math. Lunch will come at 12:00, and you will go to physical education on Monday, Wednesday and Friday afternoons at 1:30 for a 25-minute period.

Another convention underlying opening day rituals is that of standardization. As educators, we have built ourselves a series of models to serve as reference points. We have a model of a first grader, a model of a second grader and so forth. Each model is based, so we say, on research and statistical analysis of what the average first or second grade youngster is like. This model tells us how he will behave, what his interests will be, what it is important for him to learn, how well he can read, his level of thinking and reasoning ability and what size chair and desk he will need. Some of us, who are more enlightened, realize that not all youngsters will fit the "average" model, and so we have built additional models which we call the *slow third grader* or the *gifted fourth grader.* Armed with these images, we set forth on the First Day of School to mold the youngsters in our class into recognizable facsimiles of the most appropriate model. We have a variety of blueprints (in fourth grade science, you will learn about prehistoric animals, rocks and minerals, weather, flowering plants, sound and the five senses) and a variety of tools (these are the fifth grade textbooks for English, spelling and social studies) to help us manipulate children into the proper end product. Some of us are permitted to use material from another grade level in an attempt to accommodate certain youngsters. A physically large but academically slow third grader can be given a fourth-grade desk and chair which fit him and a second-grade reading book which may or may not fit him along with the third-grade curriculum and texts in other subjects which very likely don't fit him at all. The gifted fourth grade youngster can be provided for in reading by speeding him through the fourth grade reader and then giving him "enrichment" or by putting him "in" a fifth or even sixth grade reader. In other subject areas he can be given extra projects. To this extent, the instructional program can often be modified to fit the not-average youngster. Our major concern in education is to mold the child to fit the pattern, not to alter the pattern to fit the child. Or is it?

This discussion is more than a description. Conventions employed and the behavior exhibited by educators on the first day of school are a testimonial to the underlying assumptions which are held about children and about education. To go into a fourth grade classroom which has been stocked with fourth grade textbooks, to expect to see 30 fourth grade students and to carry a planbook containing learning activities designed for "a fourth grade class," is to assume that it is both desirable and possible to cause these 30 youngsters to replicate the mental model we have built of an average fourth grade student.

A LOOK AT WHAT PSYCHOLOGY SAYS

Two contemporary psychological theories are pertinent to a discussion of what to expect from children and what to hope for from education. Jean Piaget's theory deals with the intellectual development of children. Third Force psychology, or perceptual psychology, is concerned with self-concept and the adequacy of self.

Both cognitive and affective aspects of behavior are important considerations in planning for instruction and should underly all decision making regarding program design. A brief overview of some of the concepts of these theories will serve as a necessary basis for further discussion.

Piaget's Theory of Cognitive Development[1]

According to Piaget a child does not think like an adult. He is not intellectually capable of doing so. Intelligence in an individual is developmental, with this development continuing until the point, usually during adolescence, when the individual has acquired the necessary mental framework for adult-like reasoning. There is a pattern or sequence of intellectual development, with the child passing through various stages, each stage being characterized by a particular way of perceiving and reasoning about environment and experiences. Although the sequence of development is always the same, there are individual differences in timing. Thus, the kind of thinking one child is capable of at any given point in his life depends upon his stage of cognitive development at that time, but is not necessarily identical to that of which another child of the same age is capable.

The process of intellectual development involves the construction of a succession of cognitive structures, or mental frameworks, which define the possibilities for mental activity. During his development, an individual's interaction with his environment results in new aspects of experience being incorporated into the existing mental structure thereby upsetting the equilibrium. As the old mental structure is changed to accommodate the conditions of reality being newly experienced, equilibrium is momentarily reestablished. Thus adaptation to environmental encounter causes the mental structure to change and develop, thereby permitting increasingly complex patterns of reasoning.

Four factors contribute to mental growth or the development of knowledge. The most important of these is this process of equilibration. Maturation (a kind of neurological readiness), physical experience and social experience comprise the other three factors. When a child reaches the point where he is making a new bit of knowledge or a new skill his own, he is impelled to use the knowledge or the skill over and over to the point of saturation. When he is completely comfortable with it, he can "play" with it, as when he manipulates words he has learned in order to tease or make a pun.

---

[1]Background for this discussion was drawn from the Piaget references listed at the end of this chapter.

Most children entering school are at the stage of development where they are still learning to deal comfortably with symbols, including language. Thought processes are basically intuitive as opposed to logical. At this point in his life, a child's reasoning is dominated by perception—if it looks like more, then it *is* more. Some time during the three-year period between ages five and seven, a major modification of the child's mental structure occurs. The new structure permits the child to reason logically although this reasoning still needs to be based upon concrete experiences. Abstract reasoning and the ability to consider multi-aspects simultaneously are not fully realized until the child has reached the age of about 15 or 16.

Perceptual Psychology[2]

There is general agreement among perceptual psychologists as to the primary importance of a positive view of self if an individual is to realize his potential as a human being. The enabling or disabling factor is the person's perception of himself; thus, what he is is not as important to his ability to function as what he thinks he is. An individual's concept of himself is the product of his perceptions of the way in which he is viewed and treated by others. The person who has been accepted, respected and considered capable by others is the person who will see himself as acceptable, worthy and able.

Another major concept of perceptual psychology is that of self-motivation and self-enhancement. An individual will naturally tend to select and do those things which are good for his growth. Capabilities carry with them a need to be used, and it is natural for a child to do what it is good for him to do. It is necessary for him to have opportunities for concrete experiences with things, with people and with his own feelings. Opportunities for creativity, esthetic experiences and an identification and involvement with others are vitally important. As a person approaches those experiences which he feels naturally ready for, he will find meaning, satisfaction and success. His concept of himself as able builds on success experiences.

The environment in which an individual finds himself can either foster or inhibit the growth of a positive self-concept. The crucial factor in this environment is that of social interaction. It is the quality of this social interaction which tells a person who he is and how good he is. The reaction to himself and his behavior which he perceives in others determines his reaction to himself. When this reaction is positive, his openness to new experiences and his willingness to attempt new challenges is enhanced.

---

[2]Background for this discussion was drawn from the Perceptual Psychology references at the end of this chapter.

Implications for Education

Educational practices in the United States at present take very limited advantage of these psychological concepts. There are, however, several ways in which these theories can serve as a foundation for better instructional programs. Piaget's theory provides guidelines for the sequencing of learning activities, for the readiness or timing factor in introducing new ideas and new skills and for teaching strategies or methods of instruction. Perceptual psychology can serve as a base upon which to build human interaction aspects of education, and it can provide a rationale for the type of quality of activities to be presented in the classroom.

Since intellectual development follows a sequential pattern, learning activities in school can be designed to correspond to this pattern. When a child's thinking is intuitive and governed by perception, he can be provided with many opportunities for physical manipulation and sensory perception of objects and actions such as counting and matching. As his mental structures are modified to permit a greater degree of logical thinking, learning activities with which he is presented can begin to incorporate opportunities for logical reasoning about what is happening as he observes and acts upon his environment. Initial consonant substitution exercises and activities with rhyming linguistic patterns are examples. Later in his school experience, concepts and ideas with which he is asked to deal can be increasingly abstract and complex and can be farther removed from his actual firsthand experiences. Two- or three-step math problems and making justified inferences from reading are two such activities.

The fact that children progress along this continuum of mental development at different rates indicates the necessity for adjusting the timing for presentation of new kinds of learning activities to individual children. If a child's mental structure at a given time defines the possibilities and the impossibilities for thinking, it is, at best, unrealistic to ask him to attempt a task of which he is incapable merely because the average child of his age has developed to the point where he can handle such a task. For years educators have verbalized the concept of meeting individual differences. Yet instruction in classrooms today continues to be built around the grade-level curriculum using grade-level texts and workbooks, a practice which assumes not only uniformity of previous achievement and reading ability but also uniformity of mental structures and reasoning abilities. Such assumptions are erroneous.

Of the four factors Piaget identifies as contributing to the growth of knowledge, only physical and social experiences can be manipulated. We cannot force a child to learn. We can, however, prepare for him an environment rich with the physical and social raw materials which can contribute to his learning. The importance of providing concrete, manipulative materials and firsthand live experiences cannot be overstressed.

The quality of interpersonal relationships in the classroom should stem from the endeavor to provide an environment conducive to the growth of positive self-concepts. The way a student perceives himself and his abilities will depend in large part on the way he is perceived by his teachers and peers. A positive, supportive and encouraging atmosphere is essential. Recognition of the fact that children cannot reason with adult-like thought patterns enables the teacher to hold more realistic expectations regarding their behavioral possibilities. Realistic expectations and supportive reactions, resulting in the provision of appropriate learning activities and adequate opportunity for self-selection of those experiences which the child feels ready to attempt, will foster those success experiences so vital to the development of an enabling self-image.

The teacher endeavoring to apply these concepts soon begins to search for instructional programs and learning activities which are child-centered, which are not based on adult standards or on adult conceptions of *the* first, or third, or sixth grade youngster. The kind of instructional program required will be flexible in nature centering around the provision of alternatives. Alternatives for grouping children, for setting objectives, for organizing time and space and for selecting instructional materials and methods are characteristic of the flexibility necessary in this type of program. The ensuing chapters represent a search for alternatives and contain suggestions designed to encourage and contribute to your own search for better ways of meeting the varied and unique needs which you know you will find in your classroom.

Piaget References

Flavell, John H. *The Developmental Psychology of Jean Piaget.* Princeton, New Jersey: D. Van Nostrand Company, Inc., 1963.

Inhelder, Barbel and Piaget, Jean. *The Growth of Logical Thinking from Childhood to Adolescence.* New York: Basic Books, Inc., Publishers, 1958.

Piaget, Jean. *The Psychology of Intelligence.* London: Routledge and Kegan Paul, Ltd., 1951.

Piaget, Jean. *The Child's Conception of Number.* London: Routledge and Kegan Paul, Ltd., 1952.

Piaget, Jean. "Development and Learning" in R.E. Ripple and V.N. Rockcastle (Eds.). *Piaget Rediscovered.* Ithaca, New York: Cornell University Press, 1964.

Piaget, Jean. *Six Psychological Studies.* New York: Vintage Books, 1967.

Piaget, Jean and Inhelder, Barbel. *The Psychology of the Child.* New York: Basic Books, Inc., Publishers, 1969.

Perceptual Psychology References

Combs, Arthur W., Chairman A.S.C.D. Yearbook Committee, *Perceiving, Behaving, Becoming.* Washington, D.C.: National Education Association, 1962.

Combs, Arthur W. and Snygg, Donald, *Individual Behavior; A Perceptual Approach to Behavior.* New York: Harper, 1959.

Kelley, Earl C., *Education for What Is Real.* New York: Harper, 1947.

Maslow, Abraham H., *Toward a Psychology of Being.* New York: D. Van Nostrand Co., Inc., 1962.

Rogers, Carl R., *Freedom to Learn.* Columbus, Ohio: Charles E. Merrill Publishing Co., 1969.

Rogers, Carl R., *On Becoming a Person.* Boston, Mass.: Houghton-Mifflin Company, 1961.

How to Find Out
Key Facts About Children

2

How well do you know your students? Try this exercise in awareness. Select, from this year's class (or last year's class), a youngster whose name begins with *M*. Ask yourself these questions:

● How does he compare physically with others in his class?

● How does he compare academically with others in his class?

● What level of reading materials can he handle comfortably, without a struggle?

● What are his interpersonal relationships with others in the class, with adults in school?

● What is his father's occupation and where is he employed?

● Other than a job or housework, in what activity is his mother involved?

● What are the names and ages of his siblings?

● What relationships exist among the siblings?

● What are three typical comments his mother might make about him?

● What is his favorite free-time activity?

● How would you describe his most effective style or method of learning?

● What is his tolerance for failure?

● How would he describe the kind of person he is?

● What does he fear most?

● What is the most important thing which happened to him this year (or last year)?

● If he could have one wish come true, what would his wish be?

There are many things for you to know about each child. Each type of information is important. The wise selection of specific children for instructional groups involves more than merely understanding something of each child's physical and intellectual development. Questions such as those given above can guide you as you become aware of the various environments in which he moves, of the ways in which he perceives himself and his world and of the ways in which others react to him. All these bits of information are necessary. All of these factors, and others not mentioned here, contribute to his way of approaching and behaving in the structured learning environment we call school.

During the first days and weeks of the school year, heavy emphasis should be placed on the task of finding out about the children in your class. Becoming thoroughly acquainted with your students is, of course, an ongoing activity, but the early part of your year together can be most profitably spent in learning as much as you can about each child. Plan to have several activities each day which will give you more insight into the uniqueness that characterizes each pupil. Many techniques and devices are available for this purpose. Choose a variety of them and find the best ways of using them to provide you with the kinds of information you seek. Formal and informal instruments, standardized and teacher-made tests, objective and subjective evaluations: each can contribute important data, each should find a place in your program for getting to know your students.

ACADEMIC AND INTELLECTUAL CHARACTERISTICS

Having stressed the importance of learning as much as possible about the social and personal aspects of the child's uniqueness, we must avoid the danger of underplaying the need for adequate data about the academic and intellectual characteristics of the child. All elements contributing to the child's being are important, and a greater understanding of each strengthens the likelihood of providing a growth-fostering classroom environment.

Perhaps the easiest type of data to gather about a youngster is that of academic achievement. If we want to know his skill in addition or subtraction, his ability to read and get information from printed material of a given level of difficulty, his accuracy in spelling and language mechanics or his retention of facts about some specific topic, it is a fairly simple matter to find or construct a paper-and-pencil test which will give us this information. Standardized achievement tests give us certain types of general data about a youngster and may serve as a beginning step in exploring his academic characteristics. More detailed data about specific academic skills and knowledge can be obtained from teacher-made tests such as the one shown in Figure 2-1. This test was designed to be administered to a large group for the purpose of learning about individual and whole class skills in multiplication.

Multiplication Test

1.	7 x 2 =	8 x 4 =	3 x 5 =	7 x 8 =	6 x 9 =	5 x 6 =
2.	1 x 4 =	6 x 3 =	0 x 2 =	6 x 7 =	8 x 6 =	9 x 9 =
3.	8 x 5 =	9 x 3 =	6 x 4 =	8 x 8 =	6 x 6 =	9 x 7 =
4.	42 x3	542 x 2	421 x 4	70 x7	811 x 9	710 x 8
5	649 x 4	783 x 5	617 x 3	246 x 6	809 x 7	753 x 8
6.	476 x 2	923 x 4	757 x 5	684 x 9	276 x 8	543 x 7
7.	597 x24	628 x35	374 x243	839 x76	765 x87	627 x968

Figure 2-1

All examples on the lefthand side of the test deal with multiplication facts through 9 x 5. Those on the righthand side involve the "harder" multiplication facts. Rows one through three require only the ability to recall or "figure out" the multiplication fact itself. Row four calls for multiplying two- and three-digit numbers by one-digit numbers with no regrouping. Regrouping is required in rows five and six, and multiplication by two- and three-digit numbers with multiple regrouping is involved in solving the examples in the last row. In correcting the test, if a colored pen is used to indicate only correct responses, the breadth and depth of the child's ability in these multiplication tasks is quite easily visible.

Achievement is only one aspect of the academic and intellectual characteristics of students. Other considerations include the rate at which a student works and learns, his most effective mode or modes of learning and his way of perceiving and reasoning about his environment and experiences. Several possible ways of seeking information about these factors can be designed and implemented by the classroom teacher. When attempting to learn about rate and mode, it is essential that each child be given tasks at an appropriate level of difficulty. If the task is too easy or too difficult, the data you obtain about his rate or method of learning will not be of much value to you in planning his instructional program.

Rate

Two factors regarding rate will be of interest to you. How rapidly does the child complete a given task with his performance at an acceptable level? How much new learning of a given type can the child accomplish satisfactorily in a specified length of time? The following suggestions are examples of techniques you can employ to help you discover this kind of information about your students.

Prepare a series of short paragraphs at a suitable level for the child. You will need to prepare several such series in order to accommodate the range of independent reading levels in your class. List three or four questions for each paragraph calling for varied kinds of thinking. For example, one question might call for sequencing, classification or other organizational skill. One question could relate to the main idea or summarizing, which requires analysis of what has been read. A third question might ask for recall or recognition of some fact or detail in the selection. Perhaps a question involving inference or judgment would be included. Have all children begin work at a given signal. After a specific length of time, have all children stop work. The results of this simple activity will give you data not only about the rate at which a given child works, but will also provide information about accuracy and about areas of strength and weakness in reading comprehension.

Over a period of time select several exercises, both written and manipulative in nature, to be timed in the following manner. Working with a small group of about eight students, start all children on the task at the same time, allowing each child enough time to finish the entire task. Record the starting and finishing time for each student and figure a rank order rating for each. At the end of a week or two of this kind of activity, an analysis of the data should reveal some patterns with regard to rate. Exercises which might be used in this way could include the following:

- Copying a paragraph for handwriting.
- Sorting objects or pictures by class.
- Using vocabulary words in written sentences.
- Reproducing a pattern with geometric shapes.
- Using a dictionary to find meanings of words.
- Locating and labeling items on an outline map.

- Solving a set of word problems in math.
- Using a social studies book to find answers to questions.
- Weighing or measuring specified objects.
- Listing ten examples each of several categories, such as: colors, objects that begin with "s", things that are round, sounds, cities, etc.

Another method for studying a child's working rate is the use of periodic time checks. A worksheet containing many exercises of a given kind would be selected for this purpose. For instance, a sheet containing six rows of column addition, four examples to a row, could be used. Have the children work across rows doing each example in its turn. Start with a designated signal. After a given length of time, perhaps five or ten minutes, have the children make a ring around the example they are currently working or have just completed. Repeat this procedure at periodic intervals until all or nearly all children have completed the task. This technique can point up irregularities in rate such as the child who works rapidly for ten or 15 minutes and then slows down, or the one who starts out slowly and gathers momentum.

The length of time required for a child to learn new information and skills is a second important facet of rate. The use of pretests and posttests can be of value here. When new instructional material is to be presented to the youngster, a pretest designates which portions of the new material are already known to him and which portions are unknown. To find out about rate of learning, you will be concerned with that part of the new material which the child does not know or skills which he cannot perform at the onset of the new instruction. Posttests or periodic mastery tests will provide information on how much of the unknown material the child learns in a given period of time. When the instruction is of a continuing nature such as with new vocabulary words in reading, basic number facts in math or new spelling words, an average of several days' or weeks' gain in learning formerly unknown items will give a fairly good indication of rate of learning in that specific skill. The amount of new material subsequently presented to a particular child will reflect realistic expectations and will be comfortable for the child when selected on the basis of such data.

Styles of Learning

There are many ways to learn. Every child has his own composite of styles or modes of learning. One of the most exciting challenges for today's teacher is the need to provide many alternative approaches to learning which will accommodate an ever greater variety of learning styles. Finding out about the learning styles of individual children is a key factor in the diagnostic-prescriptive approach to teaching which characterizes individualized instruction.

What is meant by styles of learning? As the term is used here, it encompasses such factors as sensory modality, considerations of dependence or independence, methods of task approach, intensity of involvement, degree of passivity or activity, etc.

Some children have highly developed auditory skills. Others learn better through a visual approach, while still others may benefit most from tactile-kinesthetic activities. Generally, youngsters can utilize all of these sensory approaches to learning but may find one of them most effective in certain situations. There are many aspects of dependency or independency in learning. The degree to which a youngster prefers to work alone or to which he refers to another for help, either overtly or covertly, is one such factor. Another is the frequency of the child's need for individual help in interpreting instructions on how to do a task. Also involved is the amount of reinforcement he needs from you assuring him that he is "doing it the right way" or getting the "right" answers. Ways in which children approach tasks also differ. Some seem anxious to get on with the business, some dawdle or spend much time getting organized and ready to go and still others avoid the task in various ingenious ways. The techniques and resources employed in tackling a task will vary from child to child. For example, the first grader engaged in solving addition exercises may count on his fingers, use manipulatives such as counting blocks or an abacus, make hash-marks on a paper or rely on his memory for the required information. Children's learning styles reveal differences in the amount of involvement they feel in the learning activity, ranging from a kind of alienation or indifference to the kind of excited identification with a task which causes the youngster to turn off other stimuli and sustain purposeful concentration for long periods of time. All of these factors of learning styles are interdependent and contribute to an overall pattern with its own built-in variations for each child.

One way to study children's styles of learning is simply to present a task to several children and then watch how they go about it. The effectiveness of this technique will depend to a large extent on your choice of tasks and the methods employed in your observations. Observations must be virtually constant, impartial and not governed by preconceived notions. Some form for recording your observations is essential. The use of hash-marks on charts or continuums for each observed example of a given type of behavior might be one such method.

The type of task you assign will depend on which specific factor or factors of learning styles you wish to investigate. To investigate sensory modality, you will want to present similar sets of new material to children in each of several ways at different times—visually one day, auditorily another time, manipulatively a third day and a combination method another time. A comparison of the amount of new material learned in a given length of time by each method will give you important information about a child's perceptual strengths and weaknesses.

Other factors can be investigated through presentation of tasks similar to the following. These tasks should present a problem which the children have not yet experienced but which is not beyond their ability to solve. It should, however, be sufficiently difficult to offer a real challenge.

1. Give each child a red square, a red circle, a red rectangle, a red triangle, a blue circle, a yellow circle, a green circle, an orange circle and two loops of yarn, one red and one black, each made from a 24-inch length of yarn. Ask each child to make a circle of each loop of yarn on his desk. His task is to find some way in which he can put *all* of the red pieces inside the red loop and *all* of the round pieces inside the black loop. The solution, of course, comes when the child overlaps the loops to form an intersection of the two sets.

2. Present each of several children with a different example of a particular kind of topic, such as different cities, different countries or different industries. Have available for their use equivalent resources including books, pictures, filmstrips and/or tapes and anything else you can get your hands on. It is important that each child has access to *all* types of resources for his topic and that appropriate information is included in each type of resource. The child's task is to discover two or three (or some other specified number) important and relatively unique facts about his topic and to find some way to share this information with the group at a designated time. This time may be later the same day or on another day, but it should be announced when the task is assigned. Although resource material should be easily observable and readily accessible to all children involved in this task, the teacher should say as little as possible about them. Merely commenting that "there are several things in the room which you may use if you wish" should be sufficient. In this way, the choice of materials is left entirely up to

the child without any specific suggestions or hidden clues from the teacher.

3. Prepare for each child a package containing the following number of anagrams or letter cards:

3 a	1 f	1 l	3 p
1 b	5 g	1 m	4 r
3 d	2 h	6 n	3 t
3 e	3 i	3 o	3 u

The child's task is to form words using as many of the anagrams as he can. It is possible to use them all. One solution is shown below.

man	bed	hit	dog	fun
rag	red	pig	hop	rug
tan	ten	pin	log	run

4. Each child should be given a collection of objects or pictures or words. All collections would be exactly alike. A collection of pictures might include items similar to these.

adult dog	puppy	goldfish
red rose	kitten	yellow zinnia
adult cat	robin	violets
yellow rose	red zinnia	turtle
lion cub	white daisy	giraffe
red petunia	butterfly	ant
tiger	cow	horse
sheep	lamb	white zinnia

The child is asked to put the items into groups or sets so that all members of a set will be alike in some way. The items should lend themselves to a variety of possible classification schemes. After he has classified the items, have him explain to you the criterion for each of his sets. Then encourage him to further break down his classes or find other ways of grouping the items.

5. The plastic pieces from a ^{R} Pythagoras* puzzle or a set of cardboard shapes like those shown in Figure 2-2 is given to each child and he is asked to form a square by using all the pieces. As he finishes this task, he is asked to use all the pieces to form a rectangle. He may then be asked to use all pieces to form a shape that looks something like a house, an animal, a number such as 3 or 2 or a ship. Have him show you how his arrangement represents the shape you requested.

---

* ^{R} Pythagoras is a Kohner Bros. product.

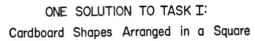

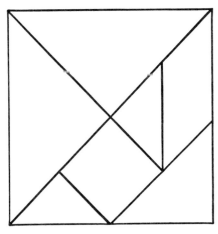

Figure 2-2

The five suggestions given above are merely illustrative of the types of tasks which could be used in studying styles of learning. Most have many possible solutions. As you observe the children carrying out their work, look for indications of the various factors of learning style discussed earlier in this section of the chapter.

Dependence-Independence

Is he quick to say, "I don't get it" when given a new task?
Does he look to his peers for direction, ideas and answers?
Does he seek frequent reassurance during the course of his working on a task?

Task Approach

How long does he take to get started on a task?
To what extent is he willing to attempt new and different tasks?
What is his tolerance for frustration?
Does he seem to have a propensity for failure?
Does he exhibit rigid mindset when tackling a problem or does he think divergently and creatively?

Involvement

What is his attention span for various kinds of tasks?
Is he generally easily distracted by sounds or movements?

Does he verbalize excitement or interest in the problem solving activities?

Does he prefer to engage in one type of activity to the exclusion of others?

Passivity-Activity

Does he sit and do nothing when he is unsure of how to proceed or when he has finished with one task?

Does he try only one source, only one possible solution, or does he explore alternative possibilities?

Can he "take off" on his own once he has been given initial direction?

Sensory Modality

Does he consistently turn to one type of resource for information or consistently avoid one type?

Does he find it difficult to attend to oral directions?

Does he frequently use reversals in writing or reading?

By what method of sensory perception does he seem to achieve the greatest success in approaching learning tasks?

Cognitive Development

Piaget's work provides a series of model tasks for identifying cognitive development as well as a pattern of sequential development against which to compare the child's performance on these tasks. The tasks are presented to each child individually but are quickly and easily administered. You may find several youngsters in a class to whom you wish to administer one or more tasks, but will probably not find it necessary to do this with all your students. When you have questions about the way a child thinks and reasons, you will find it worth the few minutes it takes to explore this important factor. Suppose, for example, that you would like to determine whether or not a child's reasoning is still at the intuitive or perceptual level. Here are a series of Piaget-based tasks which you might present to a kindergarten, first- or second-grade youngster in a single ten-minute session.

Show him a box of 20 red cubical blocks and say, "I am going to make a train. These are the cars for my train. Watch me while I make a train." Arrange 11 of the red blocks in a row as shown below.

□ □ □ □ □ □ □ □ □ □ □

Give the child a box of 20 yellow blocks just like the red ones. Ask him, "Can you make a train with the same number of cars as my

train? Make your train have just as many cars as my train has."
Observe the way he approaches the task. If he makes his train the
same length as yours but with fewer or more blocks such as this,

he is basing his thinking on perception. It looks as long as the red
train; therefore, he thinks of it as having the same number of cars. If,
however, he uses a scheme of counting or of one-to-one correspondence and so comes up with an 11-car train, his thinking has gone
beyond merely perceptually based reasoning.

Another task employing the same materials may be used next. First
remove all the blocks from the table, putting them back into their
respective boxes. This time you make both trains so that they each
have 11 cars, spaced alike and spanning the same distance. See Step I,
Figure 2-3. Tell the child that the red train has the same number of
cars as the yellow train. Have him watch you as you spread out the
yellow train so that it is longer but still has 11 cars. Ask him, "Now
are there more yellow cars, more red cars or the same number of
yellow cars as red cars?" When he has responded, ask, "What makes
you think so?" See Step II in Figure 2-3. The child who claims a
discrepancy in the number of cars based on the length of the row
(there are more yellows) or on the compactness of the row (there are
more reds) is basing his reasoning on the way things look. The child
who says there are still the same number of yellows as reds and who
explains why by saying that "you didn't take any away" or "you just
moved them apart" or "you could put them back the way they
were," is exhibiting concrete reasoning, independent of the perceptual clues.

After returning the yellow blocks back to the position shown in
Step I of Figure 2-3 and verbally restating the equality of reds and
yellows, you may perform another transformation on the yellow
blocks, this time clustering them together in a single group (Step III,
Figure 2-3), and repeat the same questions. A third transformation
would be to cluster the yellow blocks into two small groups (Step
IV, Figure 2-3), again repeating the same questions. Responses which
are consistently based on perception indicate reasoning at the
intuitive level. Responses which are consistently acceptable indicate
reasoning at the concrete level. Responses which fluctuate may
indicate that the youngster is in a transitional stage of development.

The classic Piaget test for conservation of mass using balls of
Plasticine is another device for investigating the child's cognitive
development. In this task, the child exhibits his understanding (or
lack of understanding) of the principle that a given mass of matter, in
this case a ball of Plasticine, retains the same amount of matter even

Piaget-Based Task Using Blocks

Step I

□ □ □ □ □ □ □ □ □ □
□ □ □ □ □ □ □ □ □ □   red train
                         yellow train

"There are the same number of cars in the yellow train as there are in the red train. There are just as many cars here (point to yellow train) as there are here (point to red train)."

Step II

□ □ □ □ □ □ □ □ □ □   red train
□ □ □ □ □ □ □ □ □ □ yellow train

"Now are there more yellow cars, more red cars or the same number of yellow cars as red cars? . . . Why do you think so?"

Step III

□ □ □ □ □ □ □ □ □ □   red train

□ □ □ □ □ □   yellow train
   □ □   □ □
            □

"Now are there more . . . . ?"

Step IV

□ □ □ □ □ □ □ □ □ □   red train
  □ □
  □   □   □   yellow train
□ □ □   □ □ □

"Now are there more . . . . ?"

Figure 2-3

though various transformations are made on the shape of the clay. Two equivalent balls of clay are used. One of the balls is transformed into a hot dog, a pancake and several smaller balls, using much the same procedure and line of questioning as with the blocks.

Failure to respond correctly to tests such as these indicates a student's need for additional concrete experiences with physical objects, for opportunities to observe what happens when he manipulates things and for all kinds of language-building experiences. Success with these tests probably indicates a readiness for beginning math and reading activities.

Other Piaget-based tasks test for somewhat more advanced cognitive development. Tests for conservation of liquid, conservation of volume and various tests regarding classification, are a few examples. These tasks are all simple, inexpensive and quickly administered. More detailed discussions of these and other suitable investigatory procedures and their implications are given in the Piaget references listed at the end of Chapter 1.

SOCIAL AND PERSONAL DISCOVERIES

Equally as important as information about a child's intellectual and academic characteristics is an awareness of his interests, his background and his concepts of himself and others. A child coming to school does not leave behind him his worries and concerns, his apathy or bubbling enthusiasm for life, his love or lack of it for parents, siblings and peers or his feelings about himself and the kind of person he is. All these factors contribute to the fabric of which that youngster is made. They influence or define his approaches to learning and interacting in the school setting. As you learn more about these social and personal aspects of each child's makeup, you put yourself in a better position to make wise decisions about learning programs for your students.

Finding out about social-personal factors need not be an overpowering task. Input and insight into these factors will, of course, be revealed throughout the year, but a few activities can help you concentrate your efforts toward these discoveries early in your contact with the students. Such devices as the open-ended sentence, the rating scale or continuum and the forced choice situation are valuable in seeking this kind of information about children.

The Open-Ended Sentence

For this activity, the youngster is presented with the beginnings of several incomplete sentences for which he is asked to write endings. Care should be taken in composing each "sentence starter" to provide only enough of the sentence to give it the desired direction without giving any clues or suggestions about how to complete it. There are no such things as wrong answers. Each child is asked to respond exactly as he really feels. The kind of information you seek will determine the direction in which you "point" the sentence starter. Here are examples which point in a variety of directions.

1. When I get home from school . . . . .
2. My family . . . . .
3. I am happiest when . . . . .

4. People are usually . . . . .
5. At school . . . . .
6. It is really fun to . . . . .
7. I do my best when . . . . .
8. I really don't like . . . . .
9. I wish I could . . . . .
10. It is awful when . . . . .
11. At home I . . . . .
12. The hardest thing for me . . . . .

Closely related to the open-ended sentence is the "story starter." Here the youngster is asked to write at greater length, a story or a letter or a paragraph. Story starters might include some like these.

Tomorrow is going to be a *magic* day. I will be able to do anything I want to do—all day long! . . .

Dear_____,

I want to ask you for some advice. . .

There are good things and there are bad things about school. . .

In addition to information about social-personal aspects of the child, you will also learn about his fluency in written communication, his utility of correct language mechanics conventions and his spelling and handwriting. Take note of these things but do not comment on them if you wish the youngster to continue to be open and uninhibited in his responses in similar future activities. If you suspect severe social-emotional problems you will want to refer these children to the school psychologist, guidance department, the building principal or other suitable pupil personnel services. Do not ignore signs of problems. They have a way of growing rather than disappearing.

The Rating Scale or Continuum

The use of a rating scale or continuum is common practice when seeking opinions from adults. Adapting these formats for use in finding out about children's opinions is primarily a matter of choice of vocabulary and choice of topics. To investigate how your students "feel" about various aspects of school work, you might prepare a rating scale such as this.

	Let's Have More	It's Okay	Not So Good	Very Bad News
Mathematics				
Reading				
Social Studies				
Homework				
Special projects				
Job sheets				

For very young children or those who cannot read, a rating scale with very happy to very sad faces may be given to the child. As the teacher orally gives each entry, the youngster marks the face which shows how he feels about that particular thing.

The use of a 4-point rather than a 5-point scale means that children cannot choose the midpoint. Each one must select some degree of pro or con for every entry. However, in this case he is limited to four choices. A continuum provides an opportunity for finer gradations of opinions since the child may indicate his reaction to each entry at any point on the continuum. The same types of entries may be used.

For example:

	I like it very much	I dislike it very much
Science	._____.
Spelling	._____.
English	._____.
Independent study	._____.
Working with a partner	._____.
Art corner	._____.

A rating scale or continuum may also be used to explore other kinds of interests. Entries might include some similar to these.

● Outdoor sports and games
● Being with my brother(s) and/or sister(s)

- Going grocery shopping with my mother
- Watching television
- Helping at home
- Reading a library book
- Thinking
- Choosing my own clothes
- Being by myself
- Trying new things
- Talking with my father

The Forced Choice Situation

Requesting a youngster to mentally choose between opposite or disparate alternatives can be very revealing. Choices may also be required between two or more relatively agreeable or relatively disagreeable alternatives. Forced choice situations may be presented in different ways. One is simply to list pairs of alternatives and have the student circle one of the two which he would prefer if he had to choose one.

- Watch television or play outdoors
- Take a trip to Disneyland or get any pet you would like
- Go to the library or visit your friends
- Wash dishes or clean your room
- Read a science book or do a science experiment

A second method involves presentation of three alternatives from which the youngster is to select a first choice and a second choice.

For your birthday:	Invite one special friend for dinner
	Have a few friends spend the day with you
	Have a big birthday party
Today in school:	Have a reading lesson
	Do a math assignment
	Write a story
On a weekend:	Go to the circus
	Take a special boat trip
	Go camping
Tonight:	Eat at a restaurant
	Buy a new game
	Be given a dollar

On a sunny afternoon: Weed the garden
                          Take a nap
                          Write a letter

Still another approach is to have the student provide his own alternatives. He may first be asked to list his five favorite fun-time activities, his three most precious possessions, the two people he likes most to play with, five home chores he least likes to do, etc. He is then asked to make choices in this way. If you would never again be able to do three of the five fun-time activities, which three would you eliminate? If you could only keep one of your three precious possessions, which would it be? If one of your friends were going to move away to Australia, which one would you want to go? If you had to select two of the home chores to do regularly, which would you decide to do?

Observations

Specifically planned observations provide still another avenue for investigating social-personal characteristics. Select one or two children at a time and give special attention to their activity and behavior throughout a full day. Watch them in their casual interaction with their peers when they first arrive in the morning, at lunch and during any other free time they may have during the day. Structure opportunities to observe them working and playing (in small and large group activities and discussions), and involve them in situations where they work alone. Provide time for a scheduled interview with each youngster and allow plenty of opportunity for him to give the conference direction, letting him do the talking and letting him select the topics.

Keep records of all these various kinds of observations and add this information to the other data you are collecting about the children. One way to do this would be to keep anecdotal notes. Another method would be to prepare a duplicated form for checking or indicating with symbols specific types of information. Possible entries might include items similar to the following:

Peer Interaction

☐ Approaches peers ☐ Accepts peers ☐ Rejects peers
☐ Prefers boys ☐ Prefers girls ☐ Works/plays with either
☐ Shares ☐ Hoards ☐ Loner ☐ Aggressive
Other:_____

Language Patterns

    Vocabulary: ☐Advanced ☐Average ☐ Limited
    Speech: ☐Fluent and clear ☐Speech problem
               ☐Baby talk
    Speaks in: ☐Complete sentences ☐Phrases ☐Words
    Comment:_____

General Comments and Observations

_____
_____

Taken all together, the input about academic and intellectual factors and the discoveries about social-personal characteristics will provide you with quite a detailed, but by no means complete, picture of the various students with whom you are working. You can't know too much about them. Everything you can learn about these youngsters will help you in setting objectives and establishing grouping patterns for instruction.

Developing a Framework
for Differentiated Learning
Programs

3

The teacher interested in individualizing instruction needs guidelines and a sense of direction just as any other teacher does. An organized approach to providing variety within an overall unity is required. Toward this end it is necessary to consider the characteristics of individualized instruction and to develop a method for constructing a framework for planning for such instruction.

There is more to individualized instruction than one-to-one teaching and independently pursued assignments. Tutorial situations and independent study are included in individualized programs, but these should not become the sole methodology for such programs. Often several students will profit from the same activity even though the type of benefit each reaps may vary. Large groups as well as small groups have a place in individualized programs. Whole class activities provide opportunities for participating in a unified effort toward a common goal and establish a setting for individual contributions to and interaction with large groups. Thus, an individualized program is characterized by flexibility in grouping of students who work with the teacher or with each other on short term or continuing bases.

Educators have been known to comment that in such-and-such a school or classroom or with such-and-such a teaching team, there is a totally individualized program of instruction. Investigation is likely to reveal that each youngster is moving along at his own rate and at his own level in some textbook series program or in some commercially published multilevel and often self-correcting set of materials. The teacher or teachers are available to give individual assistance as it is needed, to hold conferences, to administer mastery tests and to direct the student to the next stage of the program. It is even possible that the child's entire program is diagnosed, prescribed and monitored by a comprehensive management system. While these practices may contribute to individualized instruction, they do not in and of themselves provide it. The textbook series, the multilevel set of materials and the monitoring program can serve as valuable resources for the teacher but are limited in their value as the *governing* structure for instruction. The nature of these kinds of programs is such that only those variables which can be objectively reduced to paper and pencil and programmed into a machine or a book are taken into consideration when mapping out a study plan for a student. If rate, level and unachieved skills were all we need to consider in planning for learning, then we might be justified in relying on these highly structured guides for determining instructional patterns. Bear in mind that there is no attempt here to suggest that the teacher should not use textbook series, multilevel materials and programmed approaches to instruction. On the contrary, that is exactly what she should do—*use* them, but not submit to them.

If one-to-one instruction, independent study or multilevel and programmed materials do not define individualized instruction, what does define it? Perhaps the most satisfactory way to reduce the concept of individualization to words is to say that it is achieving the best possible match between a youngster's needs and the activities we provide for him to pursue. Total individualization assumes that it is possible to accurately diagnose all of the unique needs of each youngster and that it is possible to have available all the various kinds of activities which might conceivably be of value. Neither assumption is reasonable. So it becomes necessary in providing for individualized instruction to get the most mileage we can from what we know and have or can contrive to get. This task can be approached through the design and utilization of differentiated learning programs.

The very nature of a differentiated learning program is one of diversity. Since the program is by definition differentiated and the goal is to *individualize* as much as possible the mix of instructional ingredients, the task of presenting a neat program outline for teachers to follow becomes unrealistic. However, the necessity for some kind of framework around which to build is obvious.

BUILDING THE FRAMEWORK

A whole new era of architectural design opened up with the advent of steel cage construction. The possibilities for height, shape and utilization of interior space were greatly increased. Steel became the basic ingredient for the supporting framework of the building. In designing a building, an architect strives to achieve functional utility, beauty and individuality and takes into account such factors as available land space and technological know-how and limitations. The specific size and shape of a given building depends on the quality and arrangement of the steel grid. A wide variety of coverings—brick, glass, plastic, etc.—can be "hung" on the framework, but the building does not depend on these coverings for its structural support.

The teacher can be seen as a kind of educational architect. The increased use of statements of learning objectives as a basic ingredient for the structural framework for instructional programs has opened up a new era of possibilities for program design. Choice of subject matter or units to be "taught" and factual content to be "learned" are materials which may be hung on the framework but no longer serve as the support system. The size and shape of a given program will depend on modifications of the specific objectives selected to form the framework. In designing a differentiated learning program, the teacher will strive to assist each child to achieve the skills, feelings and understandings which will enable him to best utilize his own unique talents and characteristics. Thus, building the framework for differentiated learning involves identifying basic objectives and modifying, adapting or exchanging them so as to better fit specific youngsters.

Let us consider three basic objectives and ways in which they can be modified, as an illustration of possible components contributing to a framework for differentiated learning. One of these objectives involves mathematical understandings; the second is a skill objective in the language arts area and the third example relates to social-personal feelings and competencies.

Understanding Place Value

The child will gain a better understanding of place value. This is a very broad basic objective and should not be confused with what is commonly termed a behavioral objective. The heart of this objective is found in two notions: that of gaining and that of understanding. *Gaining* implies progress but does not specify how much or how fast. *Understanding* involves more than rote memorization or conditioned responses.

Textbook series so often indicate that in a certain grade the children will "use place value to hundreds place" or will "extend place value through six places." The devices used to teach place value include bundles of sticks, hundreds charts, expanded notation and columns labeled (from right to left) ones, tens, hundreds, etc. Often the child is considered to have "mastered" placed value when he can tell you that

$$9437 = 9000 + 400 + 30 + 7$$

or that in 852, the 5 is in ten's place. That a child really understands the purpose, value and underlying principles of place value simply because he can recite or write expanded notation, etc. is extremely doubtful. Therefore, it is necessary for the teacher to assess carefully the depth and breadth of real understanding as exhibited by the various youngsters in her room.

A middle-grade teacher may find that the children in her class fall roughly into four groups. One group may have no idea at all what place value is all about. Another may be struggling with some vague notions about it and may be able to respond correctly to the paper-and-pencil exercises from the textbook, but have trouble applying what they know (or almost know) to situations such as subtraction with regrouping. A third group in the class may have a fairly firm foundation in understanding and applying place value and need only a moderate amount of guidance in extending this application to larger numbers. Very likely some children in the class will be so comfortable in using place value that they need no help from the teacher at all with regard to place value objectives for that grade level.

Modifying the basic objective may, in this case, involve identifying four points of entry along the continuum of understanding place value and specifying expectations for progress which would be realistic for each group. Thus a framework for differentiating instruction in place value has been established. Further modifications may need to be made within the four-pronged plan as time and experience reveal the need.

Skill in Written Expression

The child will express facts, ideas and feelings in written form. Here is another very broad basic objective which leaves a great deal of room for differentiation. Modification of this objective may take into consideration such aspects of writing as language mechanics (capitalization, punctuation, usage), organization of ideas, creativity, choice of words, form, etc.

Early in the school year, a fourth-grade teacher asked her class to do some creative writing. She asked each child to write something using the words *dog, ball* and *wish.* No requirements about length or type of writing were made. Here are some of the children's responses.

Peter: See the dog
            See the ball
            I like wish

Carole: I wish the dog will bring the ball.

Steve: The little dog is brown and white and he has a red
            ball and he wishes I would play with him.

Kathy: I have a dog. Her name is Lady. She likes to play. She
            has a ball. She plays with her ball. I wish I had a cat
            too.

Julie: Roly poly dog
            Come and play with me.

            Bouncy bouncy ball
            Bounce up on the wall

            Star light star bright
            First star I see tonight
            I wish I may I wish I might
            Have the wish I wish tonight.
            I wish the sun would allways shine.
            I wish everyone would be happy.
            I wish the water would stay clean and people
            wouldn't liter.

Based on these and other samples of written work, the objectives for Peter became a four-point goal:

1. Write complete sentences.
2. Start a sentence with a capital letter.
3. End a sentence with a period or question mark.
4. Expand sentences to make them more interesting.

There were a few other youngsters in the class whose skill in written
expression placed them on a par with Peter. This formed a rather
natural group for specific instruction and practice.

Carole, Steve and Kathy varied with regard to the kind and
amount of help they needed in language mechanics. However, all
three showed a need for more creativity and expansion of ideas.
Kathy enjoyed writing, but Carole and Steve merely did what was
asked as quickly as possible so as to get the job over with. Thus,
while a common need made it possible to group these three students
together, some variation in objectives required more individualized

attention. The resulting modifications to the basic objective are shown in the following diagram:

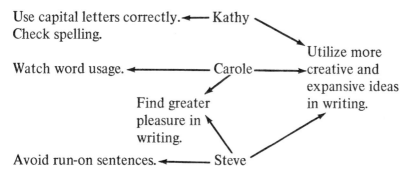

Julie needed to proofread to check for spelling and to give attention to punctuation in her poetry. Other than for these technical points, the objective for Julie centered around trying out various forms of writing such as poetry, essays, factual articles and short stories and reading examples of these by well-known writers.

The basic objective for skill in written expression did not lend itself to a few small groups with similar specific needs as readily as did the basic understanding of place value objective. However, in planning activities to work toward the various adaptations of the writing objective, it was often possible for several children to form short term groups for specific instruction. Also, it was frequently possible to initiate a common activity in writing, although expectations, individual points of concern and follow-up procedures differed.

Cooperative Group Membership

The child will work cooperatively with others as a contributing member of a group. Children vary in the roles they adopt in group activities. Some quite readily—even aggressively—assume a leadership role. Some are able to make worthwhile contributions to the group endeavor without becoming involved with leadership or organization, and others appear uncertain about what to do or say or about how to become involved. One or two may be so withdrawn or quiet and noncommunicative as to be overlooked in a group. A few may be found who actually interfere with the group activity either because of an unwillingness to cooperate or because of a propensity to "fool around" and not settle down to the business at hand. Specific modifications of the basic group membership objective will naturally take into account these varied characteristics of individual students.

The youngster who seems to take over and run the group may need to be encouraged to let others have the opportunity to be group leader. The same youngster may also benefit from learning to be a better organizer of the group endeavor. He may need to refine his skills in human relations so as to bring out the best effort from each member of his group. Chances are that an emergent group membership objective for this youngster could incorporate all three of these modifying specifications.

A primary concern for the contributing but nonleader type of group member may be the gradual assumption of some leadership activities. Perhaps such a student might strive to help the group avoid getting off on tangents by bringing attention back to the appointed task when necessary. Or he might make it his business to draw out unresponsive or unwilling members, attempting to include them in active participation.

Modification of the basic objective for other specific youngsters would also depend upon their current group membership behavior. The confused or uncertain youngster may want to concentrate on clarifying the purpose of the group activity. The shy or quiet student may feel he has nothing worthwhile to contribute. He may benefit from being encouraged to find ways in which his particular strongest talent—whether it be reading, math, drawing, good handwriting or something less academic—could be best utilized for the group endeavor. The reluctant member and the easily distracted or "clowning" pupil may also need to be encouraged to analyze their own unique strengths, interests or talents and to find ways of putting these to work for the benefit of the group activity. Although each of these various youngsters may be concentrating on different types of specific goals, these goals are all related to the basic objective of cooperative, contributing group membership.

WITHIN THE FRAMEWORK OF A CURRICULUM GUIDE

Frequently, teachers find that today's instructional programs are dictated by a collection of state syllabi, district curriculum guides and published textbook series. All too often, such program outlines continue to be based on the concept of factual content as the supporting structure of an instructional program. The teacher who finds that she must adhere to this type of curriculum guide is more limited with regard to the kinds of alternatives she can provide for a class than is the teacher who has greater options for exercising professional judgment. However, some provisions for differentiated learning can be made within the framework of the mandatory syllabus without being completely subversive.

The questions *What? How much? How?* and *So what?* suggest some of the possibilities for differentiating the instruction outlined in these guides. Most curriculum guides indicate in some way that the teacher is not expected to cover all aspects and all activities of the program with every child. For example, a curriculum guide may require that a unit on "Community Helpers" be taught during the first grade but give the teacher certain choices with regard to which specific community helpers will be considered, how much time will be devoted to the study and which activities will be employed. Thus a teacher may modify specific objectives of such a program according to such dimensions as scope and depth of content, method of study, utilization of factual material—the follow-up or *So what?* aspect of the study—or a combination of these dimensions.

For many teachers who feel that individualization of instruction is a wonderful idea, "but how do I go about it?", differentiating a program within the framework of a curriculum guide may be a comfortable first step into an unknown and mysterious-looking land. For others, who are frustrated because they are under pressure to follow a syllabus or use a particular textbook, this approach to differentiation may offer a partial escape from bondage. Suggestions for modifying two specific program outlines are discussed below and illustrate ways in which room for flexibility can be found.

A Social Studies Syllabus

One state syllabus* in social studies calls for a comparative study of communities during third grade. Types of communities have been selected on the basis of geographical-climatic characteristics. Each unit contains suggestions for specific regions to be studied, as, for example, the Amazon, the Congo, Central America and Indonesia for the study of tropical rainforest communities. A rather extensive list of print and nonprint student resource materials is included. Objectives for the unit are categorized according to geography, social organization, economic organization and political organization. Several major factual understandings with various subconcepts comprise the objectives for each section of the unit. In the tropical rainforest unit, much of the section on economic organization centers around the banana industry of Central America and wet rice agriculture in Southeast Asia.

Taking just this one aspect of the course outlined in the syllabus, let us consider ways in which learning objectives can be differentiated. There are at least three avenues for arriving at such alternatives.

---

*New York State syllabus for Social Studies, Grade Three.

Objectives can be varied with regard to the scope, depth and specific content of factual understandings. Ways in which youngsters will seek information can also vary. A third area for modification of objectives may be found in methods to be employed in recording and reporting findings.

Major factual understandings, subconcepts and suggested regions for study offer considerable leeway for scope, depth and content differentiation. Objectives for some youngsters might touch on all of the major understandings, including a few selected subconcepts, and center around a study of two specific regions. Other youngsters might be asked to deal with only one of the major understandings, but to go into greater depth involving all of the subconcepts for that one aspect of the unit, and might limit the study to a single tropical rainforest region. A third group could be concerned with all major understandings, subconcepts and suggested regions as outlined in the syllabus. A few students could be asked to extend their study beyond that outlined, to include in-depth studies of other important industries of tropical rainforest regions or case studies of specified communities.

Options for alternatives can also be found in the lists of student resource materials. Much of the printed material available on these topics is above the third-grade reading level, which limits its use to a relatively small portion of a third grade class. Selections taken from some of the easier reading materials can be used independently by some youngsters. Others may be able to gain some degree of comprehension if the material is presented to them much as a conventional reading lesson is taught—with vocabulary development, silent reading for a purpose, discussion questions and oral reading of selected passages from the material. A few students will be able to handle more advanced reading material with a minimum of teacher guidance. Many will not be able to use the print resources at all satisfactorily. These children may be reached through more extensive utilization of films, filmstrips, flat pictures, etc. Specific objectives related to ways of seeking information should take into account the child's style of learning and reading level and the characteristics of the resource materials and learning activities available.

Recording and reporting of information and of the results of study can be accomplished in many ways. Written records can take the form of outlines, charts, tables of information and word lists. Reports can be written as simply as a sentence or two or may be as complex as a beginning form of term paper. Recording information and making reports can be done orally. This may involve the use of tape recorders or may be done "live." Oral reports can be given to a small group of children, to a larger audience or in a one-to-one conference with the teacher. Sending a youngster to the librarian, the principal or another teacher to "tell her what you found out about . . ." constitutes a kind of informal oral reporting. A third method for recording and reporting involves the preparation of visuals such as maps, murals, dioramas, transparencies, graphs, models, etc. Project work such as this is always a favorite activity. The type of project, the scope and depth of factual information needed and teacher expectations regarding the final product provide variables for differentiating objectives for this form of activity.

Curriculum Guide for Science

In one school district, a science curriculum committee prepared a curriculum guide for the elementary teachers of the district. The program was based on six units: astronomy, plants, animals, earth science, physical science and the human body. Each unit was presented every year with new material being included in a kind of spiral curriculum fashion. Objectives were given in terms of factual content to be learned. Suggestions for demonstration "experiments" and a few pupil activities were included with each unit, together with a bibliography of various science textbooks and trade books containing related material. Some audio-visual materials were also listed.

One fourth grade teacher found that the children were bored with the repetition and the passive approach to learning fostered by this program. She felt frustrated by the sterility of the program and yet felt obliged to cover the material contained in the curriculum guide. In analyzing the most pressing weaknesses of the program, she decided to attempt to find ways to:

1. Avoid repetition of content material which children already knew.

2. Involve the children more actively in the learning process—to get away from telling, reading and explained demonstrations as the means of learning facts.

3. Expand the program to include specific interests of the children.

Toward this end she devised the following three-phase plan. First, she gave the children a paper-and-pencil test covering all the factual information contained in the objectives for a given unit. From the results of this test, she prepared for each child a list of unit goals in the form of questions. For every factual objective which he didn't "know" on the pretest, he was given a written question. It was then his task to find and write the answer to each question, have its accuracy checked by the teacher and be responsible for remembering it and being able to answer it correctly on a subsequent test. A variety of textbooks, trade books and audio-visual material was made available in the classroom for this purpose.

The second phase of the plan was the provision of opportunities for experimentation and project activities related to the unit. Questions and suggestions were printed on cards and posted on a bulletin board. Materials for carrying out these activities were assembled on a table beneath the bulletin board. When a given activity related specifically to one of the goal questions of a particular child, this activity was added to his list and became one of his objectives for the unit. Each child was expected to carry out a specified number of these activities, at least some of which were of the pupil's own choice.

Phase three of the plan related to expanding the program to include special interests. During each unit, each child was asked to identify some area in which he was interested and to do a project in this area. The project could be in the form of an experiment, a report (written or oral), a diorama, a bulletin board, etc. For those children who could not identify a project of special interest, a variety of suggested activities was available from which he could choose.

The special project activity was added to the child's list of unit goals. Each week the teacher made a "progress check" of each child's activity during that week. At this time, spot checks of goal questions would be given orally and at random.

Although this program did not deviate very far from the curriculum guide, it did represent the teacher's first steps toward differentiation in science instruction and as such became a milestone. The children were, without exception, enthusiastic. They spent more time and energy on science than they previously had. When the final examination was given, covering the factual material required in the units, not one child failed.

Summary

Objectives are the stuff of which a framework for differentiated instruction is made. Basic objectives provide a unity for the program. Modifications to the basic objectives provide a structure for variation. The specific form a modified objective takes for a given youngster depends upon that child's behavior at any given time as observed and interpreted by the teacher. A child's current behavior reflects interrelationships among various factors, including his cognitive capacities and his feelings about himself, his environment and others. The collection of specific objectives for a particular youngster or group of youngsters defines the possibilities for the shape and size of an instructional program.

Variations in these collections of objectives call for variations in instructional approaches and content. Even within the framework of curriculum guides and syllabi may be found possibilities for these variations. Variations in objectives, in instructional approaches and in content comprise the differentiated learning program.

Establishing a Provocative Learning Environment

4

Time was when preparing the classroom meant lining up the desks and chairs, stocking the shelves with 30 each of the various textbooks and workbooks, mounting the alphabet cards above the chalkboard and putting up a bulletin board. The lucky ones also needed to place the extra table and the record player in appropriate locations. Thus the environment was prepared in which the teacher could do her teaching.

Today we are more inclined to think of the classroom as a setting in which the children can do their learning. When differentiated learning objectives form the basic structure for the program, flexibility and organization become keystones in the establishment of the learning environment. Flexibility in the use of physical, human and nontangible components of the environment makes it possible to get greater mileage out of whatever resources are available. Organization helps to maintain order where chaos could easily sabotage the whole operation. These two considerations—flexibility and organization—serve as the guiding principles for all aspects of the planning and establishment of an environmental setting for differentiated learning.

Preparing and maintaining a setting conducive to varied learning involves consideration of such physical aspects of the environment as use of space, storage facilities, arrangement of furniture and equipment and provision of instructional materials and supplies. Human, or psychological, aspects of environment must also be taken into account. The physical environment can be thought of as those tangible *things* which are there even when no person is in the room. The psychological environment consists of a conglomerate of feelings and attitudes constituting a kind of intangible *atmosphere* which pervades the room when teacher and students are there. This atmosphere involves mental and emotional reactions and interreactions to the things, the people and the events occurring in the setting. A consideration of various components of the physical environment is contained in this chapter. Chapter 5 deals with psychological and intangible aspects of classroom environment.

The gross physical space allotted to a teacher is still likely to be a self-contained classroom. Many of the new schools being built are incorporating concepts of flexible space and open space, but the majority of teachers today will find themselves and their 30 students housed within nonacoustical walls, four-square, containing such permanent fixtures as a blackboard, windows, one door to the hall, bulletin boards, probably some kind of storage facility and (hopefully) a sink. Within this "stage," the teacher creates the environment for learning. She may feel restricted by the type and amount of things available for furnishing and stocking this room. Ingenuity and a large supply of derring-do can help to overcome limitations in the physical aspects of stage setting. The teacher who is setting the stage for differentiated learning will need to provide space and facilities which permit various kinds of activities to go on simultaneously much of the time.

There's Never Enough Space

Classroom space seems to diminish as physical activity increases. Thirty children and 30 desks are much more compact when the children are folded neatly into their desks, but active involvement in learning and differentiated learning activities are not readily available to neatly folded and stored children. So you feel the need for more space. Fortunately there are ways in which to ease the space squeeze. They all involve better utilization of the space which you already have.

Divide and Conquer

The first step toward organization of space is the division of space, and, as strange as it may seem, the division of space can also increase its flexibility. A little wand waving and simple maneuvering can conjure up an alcove and one or two nooks and crannies in a basically rectilinear classroom. Folding screens and portable hardboard panels in freestanding frames provide ready-made partitions. A double row of student desks face-to-face and placed at right angles to the wall designates an alcove-like area on either side of the row. See Figure 4-1.

Furniture Clusters Divide Space

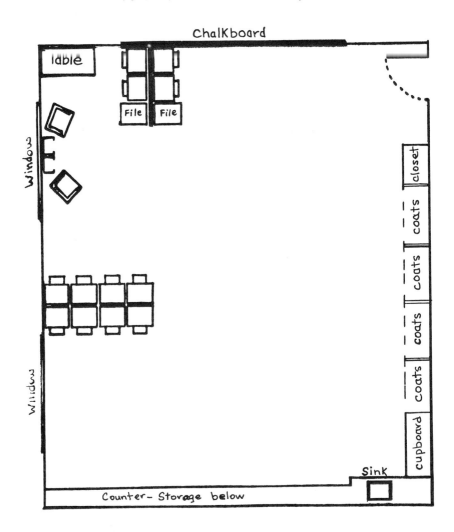

Figure 4-1

Figure 4-1 also shows how two filing cabinets placed end-to-end and a large piece of heavy cardboard or Homosote (held in place by the filing cabinets) can create further division of space into quiet study areas for two pairs of student desks. By placing this unit perpendicular to the front wall of the classroom, additional privacy and seclusion is obtained for a reading corner. Twelve student desks, a reading lounge and a 9-foot square area of unfurnished space tucked away in a corner occupy approximately one-third of this classroom.

Spatial divisions can also be designated by materials hung from the ceiling. A length of burlap weighted at the bottom with a dowel rod can be used for an ongoing stitchery project or as a background for displaying smaller stitchery work, as well as serving to partition space. A split-reed porch shade can be rolled up when not used as a space divider. When a temporary division of space is desired, short scraps of colored, flame-proof crepe paper tied at 6-inch intervals to floor-length pieces of twine weighted with metal washers provide a quick and inexpensive see-through wall which the children will enjoy making.

Multipurpose Space

Make a given area of space serve several purposes. Turn one corner of the room into a "wet" area. Locate it near the sink, if you have one. This area can be used as an art studio, a science lab or a project workshop as the need arises. Lengths of oilcloth can be spread out on desks, tables or the floor for work surfaces which also catch spills and simplify clean-up. Another space, occupied by a large table or a cluster of six or eight student desks can also serve a variety of purposes. You might use it as a place to meet with reading groups, for small group instruction in math, as a center for discussion groups or group projects, or, by wheeling up a specially outfitted A-V wagon, turn it into a listening and/or viewing station. A very tiny multipurpose space with a single student desk or small table can be tucked into a sheltered corner or behind a three-fold screen. Use this space for pupil-teacher conferences, for a quiet place for creative writing or solitary meditation. A youngster could find privacy here for taking a test or a nap, for working on an important task or for just getting away from it all for awhile. This space should be known to all as a stay-away-I-want-to-be-alone spot.

Found Space

Engage in a little divergent thinking and you may find extra space you didn't think you had, especially storage space for some of those hard-to-store or seldom-used items. Where *do* you put all those bulky paintings you are saving for the school's clothesline art show next May? Perhaps you can steal 2 or 3 inches from the back wall of the pupil's wardrobe. Securely fasten together the cover and bottom of a heavy duty suitbox obtained from your local department store and cut away one of the short, narrow ends of the box, making the cut-away part lower in the front than on the sides and back. Hang the box along the wardrobe wall by suspending it from coat hooks or by using a carpenter's staple gun. Use the space to store charts, posters, children's drawings, large mounted pictures, etc. You may be able to steal a bit of space from the inside of cupboard or closet doors in much the same way.

Many classrooms have rather high ceilings. Is there any way you can salvage some of this unused space? With permission and perhaps a little help from your custodian and a couple of pulleys, you may be able to devise some overhead storage bins. If you can't look up for extra space, look down and find room to tuck away two or three children from time to time. When you are not using your desk, the knee hole area makes a delightful hideaway for one youngster who wants some peace and quiet while he studies his spelling words or works on a brainteaser. That 2-by-4-foot extra table in the corner which holds your class library has room underneath for a small rug and some cushions where two children can read orally to each other, practice with math flash cards or listen to a story record with earphones.

If you are willing to spend a little time and a few dollars, here is a project for you and your class which will give you many dividends. Buy a 4 by 8 sheet of ¾" plywood finished on one side. Sand, and if desired, paint with floor enamel the four edges and finished side of the panel. Apply two or three coats of a hard coat, high gloss varnish or gym floor seal to the painted surfaces. Ask the manager of a floor covering store to give you old carpet samples and scraps left from carpet installations. Parents may also be able to supply carpet scraps. Have the children create an interesting mosaic design using the carpet pieces and glue or staple them to the unfinished side of the plywood. Now you are ready to install and enjoy your finished project.

Create a raised platform by supporting the panel on concrete blocks or large kindergarten building blocks, and suddenly you have divided space, multipurpose space and salvaged storage space all in one small area. Underneath the platform is room to store such items as . . .

- one or two painting easels
- 20 feet of unfinished mural, rolled up

- a box of costumes for impromptu dramatizations
- the floor-model large chart holder
- a folded card table
- three-dimensional art projects (for that May art show)
- those huge consonant posters (when you aren't using them)
- a folded puppet theater
- extra floor cushions
- a roll of butcher paper or extra packages of large-size newsprint.

Whenever possible, store the items in large blanket boxes, under-bed storage boxes or on large sheets of cardboard to provide easy access to the stored materials.

With the carpeted side up, the unit becomes . . .

- a seating platform for story hours, small group instruction, filmstrip watching, discussion group session, interest club meetings, listening to records, sitting cross-legged and visiting or reading or just plain relaxing
- a place to play house or serve "tea"
- a reading lounge
- a place to lie down and solve problems (math problems and word riddles mounted on the ceiling overhead) or watch the mobiles suspended from above.

Flip over the panel and with the hard surface side up you have . . .

- a stage for playlets, concerts and variety shows
- a place to make a store, bank, factory, library, newspaper office, travel agency, television studio, etc.
- a picnic table or luau platform
- space for a mini art gallery, museum, flower show, science fair, zoo or other exhibit
- a place to play with checkers, jacks, dominoes, puzzles, etc.
- a bench for 18 students
- room to create and operate a snack bar
- a work surface for lots of small projects or for one or two large projects
- a place to build a walk-in diorama or a store window to decorate
- support for one huge three-dimensional map, village or scenario from another land.

If desired, the panel may be supported by four student desks when you wish to raise it temporarily to a more comfortable working height. Have plenty of oilcloth covers to protect the panel when using it for wet or messy projects.

The children will dream up dozens of ways to use this unit. You will find it almost constantly in use—certainly worth the time and effort you spend making it!

Furniture and Equipment

Inseparable from considerations of the division and flexible utilization of space is the problem of furnishing and equipping the classroom. Minimum essentials are generally considered to be a desk and chair for each person in the room. The teacher who is also provided with two extra tables, a few extra student chairs and a filing cabinet considers herself fortunate indeed. In planning the arrangement of a classroom to provide a setting for many kinds of simultaneous activities and various sizes of groups, it soon becomes apparent that there is a need for other items of furniture and equipment than are generally available. Solutions to some of these problems may lie in looking for better ways to utilize the things which are available as well as searching for ways to supplement them. In either case, organization and flexibility are essential characteristics to be considered.

One of the first things to do is consider various ways for using student desks. If you can stop thinking of them as being things you assign to children to serve as a home away from home, you will open up possibilities for greater flexibility. Consider these desks as modular components to be used in assembling learning stations of various sizes and for various purposes. Arrange desks in one area to serve as a location for small group instruction. A second cluster of desks can be used for independent study and cooperative work on "quiet" tasks. Another station may be designated for more active projects which require more discussion and moving around. Here and there one or two desks may be used for study carrels or as a place for two students to work together. One station may serve as a media center where record player, filmstrip viewers, cassettes, listening post and corresponding supplies are used. When you wish to meet with the whole class, use the station which has the greatest number of desks, bringing extra chairs to the area. And there is always the floor! Children use it quite spontaneously when given the opportunity.

Supplementing classroom furnishings creates a real challenge for the teacher. Such endeavors are likely to be made up of equal parts of ingenuity, work and scrounging. Take, for example, the case of the ubiquitous orange crate. Give some creative thought to ways in which orange crates may help to solve some of your furniture problems. "Scrounging" for orange crates is largely a matter of making a few trips to see the produce manager at the supermarket. Sanding and painting will often be the only work required. Obvious uses include bookcases, filing boxes, toy bins, record cabinets and components for making stores, libraries, etc. Two units topped with plywood will make a study or work surface. Fasten two units side-by-side, top with hardboard and mount on casters to create an easily movable storage cabinet with work space on top. Six orange crates, a 4-by-6 sheet of plywood topped with oilcloth or vinyl tile samples and a 2-by-6 panel of pegboard will create a project activity center where several young children can work at one time. See Figure 4-2. Perhaps you might stock one side of the center with art supplies and the other side with science materials. Locate the unit near the sink or use two pails, one for clean water and one for waste, if you do not have a sink.

ART—SCIENCE CENTER

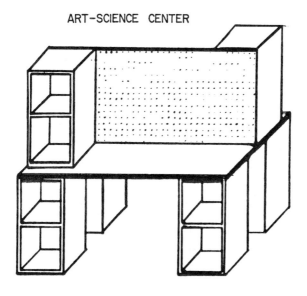

Figure 4-2

Cardboard carpentry offers an opportunity for creating and building some of your own furnishings, even if you are not especially handy. Sheets of very rigid, heavy duty cardboard which can be cut and drilled with simple carpenter's tools can be assembled to form a variety of items for classroom use. Storage units, easels, tables, study carrels, playhouses, puppet theaters and movable partitions can all be made quite easily. The students in one sixth-grade classroom made models of several items of classroom equipment, displayed them in the school lobby and filled orders for many teachers. Custom-made items were also built according to teacher designs and specifications. One such order was for a large-scale study maze for a fourth grade classroom. This structure occupied a space about 8 by 12 feet and contained eight or ten tiny alcoves, study carrels and niches for one or two students. Cardboard carpentry constructions are sturdy enough to stand up under regular classroom use for from one to three years. A structure such as the study maze could be cut and assembled by an adult in about an hour.

Improvisations are virtually as unlimited as your imagination. Assess your most pressing needs. Look around and see what can be obtained and then put your mind to work. If you can find a cooperative display manager in a local department store, you may be able to salvage all kinds of intriguing display racks and structures which can be adapted for use in your classroom. Let parents know when you need something special, like an old, comfortable chair for the reading corner. Consider the possibilities for using empty nail kegs (obtained from building supply companies or hardware stores). They can be used as the base for a small table, topped with a plywood or heavy cardboard circle. You could also use one for storing yardsticks, rolled-up posters and charts, a supply of crepe paper, wall maps, mural paper, baseball bat, etc. Or cut one in half and cover the opening with a circle of plywood—padded if possible—to create two student-size stools for placing at a small table. When kitchen counters are being installed, a section of plastic laminate-covered particle board is often cut out to accommodate the sink. With the edges smoothed down, this piece becomes a very satisfactory top for a small table. Look around you and stir up your imagination. Perhaps you will contrive to solve many of your lack-of-furniture problems in unique and unforeseen ways. Get the children involved in the search for solutions, too. They will both enjoy and benefit from trying to solve *real* problems.

Instructional Materials and Supplies

Teachers engaged in differentiating learning programs are interested in providing alternatives for students. This requires a variety of instructional materials—not just different textbooks at different levels, but also other kinds of materials. Textbooks, workbooks, audio-visual materials and manipulative objects are all part of the learning environment.

The ways in which such materials are used will differ considerably from the ways they are used for whole class programs.

Workbooks, for example, are rarely issued to students to be gone through page by page. More likely, an assortment of various workbooks will be available as resources, and a student might be assigned work from specific pages in specific workbooks according to the skill and level on which he is currently working. When used in this way, workbooks are not consumed at the rate of two or three per child per year. Budget money can be used to buy a few copies of many different workbooks and textbooks rather than many copies of one or two. In this way, a teacher has many more resources from which to choose in trying to find a good match between student and assignment.

You will naturally want to get the greatest amount of utility out of the materials you have at hand. To do this, it is important to become very familiar with the contents of these materials. Decide, specifically, what objectives can be reached by using this page or this section or this filmstrip. Be selective and use those parts of books, workbooks and audio-visuals which you think are best, and don't be afraid to ignore portions which you feel do not meet any objectives your students are working on. You will find it worth your while to keep some kind of index system on sources of practice materials for specific skills, especially those that your students are frequently involved with. An index card similar to the one shown in Figure 4-3 gives you a wealth of helpful resources at your fingertips, ready for reference at the moment the need arises.

Reading Skill Index Card

		Reading Skill:	*Bl blend*
PUBLISHER	AUTHOR	TITLE AND LEVEL	PAGES
Lippincott	Hay & Wingo	*Reading with Phonics*	54, 55
Lippincott	Wingo & Hletko	*More Sounds, Letters and Words "B"*	32, 33
Lyons & Carnahan	Halvorsen, et al.	*Phonics We Use "B"*	71
Barnell-Loft	Boning	*Working with Sounds "B"*	Unit 16
Harcourt Brace & World	Durrell & Murphy	*Speech-to-Print Phonics*	Lesson 26
Ideal	—	Magic Cards: Cons., Blends and Digraphs	ex. 2
Harper & Row	O'Donnell	Phonics Wkbk: *Real and Make-Believe*	67

Figure 4-3

Not always will you be able to find suitable materials to use for some of your objectives. In this case you may feel that the importance of the objective and the frequency of the need for the materials make it worth your while to make your own. Every effort should be made to ensure a good return for your time and work. A few simple guidelines will help in achieving this end.

First, plan the activity so that it really supports the specific objective you have in mind. If the objective relates to the short *a* vowel sound, for example, it is important to distinguish between recognizing the spoken sound of the short *a* and correctly identifying and pronouncing printed words containing the short *a* sound. For the former, an activity or a series of activities could be prepared on tape cartridges. If paper-and-pencil activities must be used for the hearing objective, pictures of well-known objects can be employed as the stimulus for deciding if the short *a* sound is heard. Instructional materials for the objective relating to reading short *a* words could utilize a tape and worksheet combination, [R] Language Master cards or paper-and-pencil activities using printed words.

Materials you make yourself should be designed to be nonconsumable whenever possible. When the child is called upon to respond in writing, plan the format of the material so that it is possible for him to write his responses on another sheet of paper, thereby leaving the original to be used again by another youngster when the need arises. Protect paper materials from tearing and smudging. Make the material (or mount it) on a heavy card stock such as oak tag. Use acetate sheet protectors or transparent adhesive vinyl to cover the material. This gives it extra strength, greater eye appeal and provides a surface which can be wiped clean. For recorded activities to be used with headsets, tape cartridges and [R] Language Master cards are easier for children to handle than tapes on reels. Be sure to take precautions against accidental erasure of your recorded tapes. Manipulative materials containing many pieces, such as sets of cards to be sorted, should have an identifying code—color, letter, number, etc.—on the back of each piece. Stray pieces can then easily be returned to the proper set of materials and sets will remain complete much longer.

Teacher-made materials planned for use in learning activities, rather than in check-up or testing activities, should be designed for independent work. Whenever possible, make it obvious to the child from the format of the material exactly what he is to do and how it is to be done. When written instructions are necessary, keep them brief, simple and very clear, using only vocabulary words which you are sure the child can handle. You may wish to use a rebus technique—the use of drawings to illustrate words—for some of the instructions. Adherence to a few basic formats which you use often will simplify the child's task of interpreting directions. Such formats could include classification, matching, sequencing, completion, multiple choice, identification or reproduction, questions to be answered, etc. Activities calling for responses which are easily identified as correct or incorrect should include some kind of feedback for the child. Answer keys printed on the back of the material, on separate cards or kept in an easily accessible place make it possible for the student to check his own work as soon as he has made his responses. Learning reinforced with immediate feedback is more effective than that utilizing delayed feedback. Materials designed in these ways to be self-directing and self-correcting enable the student to be more independent in engaging in the learning activities, a factor which also enables the teacher to utilize in-class-room time for more worthwhile activities than giving repetitious directions.

A final consideration regarding returns for your effort in making instructional materials concerns the appeal of the material. Children enjoy working with materials that are attractive to look at, pleasant to handle and fun to use. Teachers have been known to say that learning isn't always fun and we should stop trying to coddle children by attempting to make everything seem like a game. Agreed—learning isn't always fun; sometimes it is very hard work. But even hard work can be attractively packaged. Too often learning that isn't fun could, just as easily, become enjoyable. Children playing one of the *Fun with Rhymes* games or *Junior Phonetic Rummy* have just as many opportunities to practice rhyming or using vowel sounds as children working on a ditto worksheet or a page in the workbook.* Creating your own game-type learning activities brings big dividends in pupil enthusiasm and can provide valuable practice in many skills.

Paper-and-pencil worksheets can often be presented in more intriguing and appealing ways with very little extra effort. A classification exercise, for example, can be made into a manipulative activity where the child sorts word cards according to category rather than copies words into specified lists. The manipulative format calls for the same practice with reading vocabulary words and the same

---

Fun with Rhymes is a product of Instructo Products Co.; *Junior Phonetic Rummy* is a product of Kenworthy Educational Service, Inc.

thinking with regard to criteria for classification—but it is more fun to do, especially for younger children. Since these materials are being made nonconsumable, you need only one copy of any one worksheet and are therefore liberated from dependence on the duplicating machine. This permits more creativity in designing the appearance of the worksheet. For example, the exercise may be printed on colorfully illustrated sets of children's writing paper, mounted on oak tag and covered with transparent adhesive vinyl. The use of colorful felt-tip marking pens, colored paper or poster board and sketched or pasted illustrations makes the preparation of attractive paper-and-pencil activities well within the realm of every teacher's talents.

Summary

The learning environment consists of a physical setting and a psychological climate or atmosphere. Physical aspects include consideration of space, storage, furnishings and instructional materials. Flexibility and organization are of key importance in planning to utilize the physical classroom setting to create a place where differentiated learning can take place. Judicious division of space coupled with multipurpose use of a given area go a long way toward making the most of available classroom space. New ways of using standard furniture and various avenues for supplementing inadequate classroom furnishings reveal new possibilities for this aspect of the physical setting. Effective utilization of available instructional materials helps adapt them to use in differentiated learning programs. Ensuring an adequate return for the effort expended in designing and making learning materials takes into consideration such factors as frequency of expected use, suitability of material for its purpose, nonconsumable formats, self-directing and self-correcting characteristics and the appearance and appeal of materials.

Establishing Appropriate Learning Conditions

5

The physical setting, with its considerations of space, furnishings and instructional materials, provides a stage upon which to act out the school experience. A given classroom setting can be utilized in any number of ways. The way in which you and your class operate will depend upon a composite of intangible factors which make up the climate or "feeling" in the room.

One of these factors involves the network of social-personal interactions which we often refer to as the psychological atmosphere. Attitudes, opinions and feelings will very naturally have an impact on the ways you work with children and on the ways in which they function and respond. A second factor relates to the utilization of time. Scheduling, the subdivision of time into component parts or blocks, serves as a temporal framework for the activities taking place in the classroom. The grouping of children for learning activities also has its effect on the intangible climate of the room. Various grouping patterns serve differing functions and provide a wide range of possibilities for social-personal interactions. A fourth factor contributing to your *modus operandi* is that of planning. The methods you employ in planning instructional activities and other opportunities for learning will influence the "atmospheric conditions" in your classroom.

Each of these factors is interrelated. Scheduling, planning and grouping are merely different avenues for approaching the problem of staging the learning action which is to take place in the physical setting. The total procedure will stem from the way you feel about the children, which, in turn, establishes a psychological atmosphere. Taken together these factors determine how you will work with children.

THE PSYCHOLOGICAL SETTING

Psychological aspects of the environment depend more upon the teacher's self-concept and concern for others than on the paraphernalia of space, furniture and learning materials. Where the teacher feels adequate and accepted, as a person and as an educator, a growth-fostering atmosphere in which learning can take place is likely to occur. Toward this end, the teacher can analyze her own strengths and talents and explore ways in which they can best be utilized to create the desired environment. She is best able to determine the rate at which she feels able to move, in the direction of differentiated learning programs. When she feels comfortably challenged about what is happening in her classroom the children will feel comfortable and yet challenged.

The psychological setting should be one which fosters the growth of individual children in perceiving themselves as acceptable, adequate and able beings with a sense of concern for others. What are some characteristics of such an environment? In this kind of environment high value is placed on the worth of the individual, as is exhibited by the teacher who listens with both ears (and both eyes) to the child speaking to her, and who refrains from doing paperwork during show-and-tell or oral reports. An awareness of trusting pervades a growth-fostering environment. The teacher does not feel that children will "do the right thing" only when compelled by some authority symbol. A sense of "freedom to attempt" pervades this environment. This attitude is apparent in the teacher's reaction to student mistakes. Children in this kind of environment have success experiences in most of their endeavors because expectations are based on specific knowledge of individuals rather than on an adult preconception of the average ____-th grader. Children enjoy and are considerate of each other as is evident in the way they work with and for, rather than in competition with, one another. Conditions such as these are typical of a growth-fostering environment.

A Chain Reaction

There is a story about a general whose wife argued violently with him at breakfast one day. The general soon found occasion to chew out the colonel, who turned around and made life miserable for the major and so on down the line until the sergeant was unusually rough on the private. The private had to be satisfied with kicking the dog to let off steam. One wonders what the poor dog did and where it all ends. This chain reaction of anger and hatefulness stemmed from a single unpleasant encounter. By the same token, a chain reaction can be set in motion by a positive experience or encounter.

We have said that the way a child perceives himself and his environment determines his course of action. The child's behavior toward others affects their perceptions of him and of themselves, which, in turn, influences their subsequent behavior toward each other and toward the original child. Thus we have a kind of cyclical chain reaction which eventually feeds back to and reinforces the perceptions and behavior of the originator. The spiraling effect of this phenomenon can be devastating if the original perceptions were negative. It can be equally enhancing when the original perceptions are positive. Many of the child's perceptions about himself as a learner result either directly or indirectly from the interactions between himself and his teacher. Which kind of chain reaction are you setting in motion? If you truly value the child as an individual, if you respect and trust him, if you provide him with many opportunities for success experiences, if your reaction to his mistakes is one of positive support and guidance and if you exhibit toward him the good manners and consideration you expect from him, you are undoubtedly contributing to positive perceptions.

Freedom of Expression

The comfortable and supportive rapport which develops in a growth-fostering environment such as we have been describing here makes it possible to establish vehicles for easy and valuable communication. Children, like the dog in our chain reaction story, often need a safety valve for letting off steam. They need a satisfactory, yet acceptable, way to let you know how they really feel about something, or to examine uncertain and confused reactions or feelings. The growing practice of using circle sessions or circle discussions for the oral exploration of ideas and feeling in a nonthreatening atmosphere is one kind of response to this need. Many people have found that writing a letter or an editorial or essay has helped to release bottled emotions, either of joy or anger or of frustration. Writing down ideas can also help to clarify and organize confused thinking.

Opportunities for communicating feelings, suggestions and remarks should be available in the classroom at all times. One way might be to provide a *Comment Box* into which anyone may drop a written communication to the teacher. A youngster should feel free to comment about anything and express any feelings or opinions he may have. He should have the option to sign his communication or leave it unsigned. Only the teacher should have access to the contents of the Comment Box. If the child has signed his name, some kind of response should be given to him—privately when this is appropriate or openly when his communique calls for this, such as when class opinion on some topic or question is requested. In cases where the child has not signed his comment, it is most important to honor his wish to remain anonymous. You will probably know who wrote it even without his signature, but do not betray this knowledge no matter how sorely tempted. Any violation of the ground rules for the Comment Box will undermine its effectiveness. If a child feels that his written communication is urgent, he should feel free to deliver it directly to the teacher for immediate consideration.

Setting the Scene with Stories

Stories which are read aloud to the children and which are designed to trigger follow-up activities such as those discussed below can serve a valuable role in establishing a classroom atmosphere of mutual consideration and thoughtfulness toward others.

1. Discuss emotional reactions and feelings of characters in the story. Have students relate similar experiences or feelings which they have had.

2. Consider alternative ways in which certain story characters could have behaved in a given situation and how that might have changed the outcome of the story.

3. Describe a hypothetical situation involving conflict or a highly charged emotional episode and ask students how a particular story character might have reacted. Have students discuss how they, personally, might react to the same hypothetical situation.

4. Have students describe the personality of a story character. Ask them how that character might have reacted differently to a situation in the story if he had been a different type of person. Be specific—for example, ask what so-and-so might have done if he had been happy instead of sad, selfish instead of unselfish, honest instead of dishonest or tired and sick instead of healthy and energetic. Ask students how their own behavior changes when they are tired, hungry, especially happy, etc.

5. After having presented a story situation in which a character has encountered some distressing experience, have children discuss ways in which other story characters could make life more pleasant for him under the given circumstances.

6. After having read and discussed some story with a "moral," such as an Aesop's Fable, present children with another moral and ask them to write a story to go with it.

7. Give your students a quick character sketch of a hypothetical person and ask them to write a story (or draw a cartoon or comic strip) which illustrates this person's character and his probable reaction to things that happen in the story.

8. Have children discuss which things in a story made a given character feel happy and friendly. What things made him feel miserable and grouchy? Then have the children describe the kinds of things which make *them* feel happy and friendly or miserable and grouchy.

How Much Freedom? How Much Authority?

A major goal in education today is to have children develop independence and self-direction. Problem-solving and decision-making students are not those dependent upon authority figures to tell them what and when to think or do. Self-motivation, self-selection, goal setting and self-evaluation are all part of the process of self-direction. The role of the teacher is one of providing guidance, opportunities and support for self-directed learning. A teacher may provide guidance in the form of learning objectives and counsel about ways of reaching the objectives but unless the child decides within himself, "yes, I will learn this," he will not. Opportunities for learning—such as instructional materials, experiences and feedback—may be made available by the teacher, but the child must become actively involved in the process of attending to and assimilating input in order for learning to take place. Both the will to learn and active involvement in learning can be enhanced by the provision of an adequate support system. This support system is supplied by the teacher through the allotment of sufficient time, the availability of many alternative possibilities for learning and lastly through an attitude of willingness to loose the child from the bondage of total adult authority and a positive, constructive reaction to both success and failure.

Children and teachers who have been canalized into accepting a passive role for students and an imparting role for teachers will be unable to make an overnight transition to the more "open" classroom atmosphere advocated here. This does not mean that the transition cannot be accomplished; it merely means it will take awhile and may be spotted with occasional failures and discouragement. Teachers wishing to make this transition will be wise to devise some generalized plan for gradually emerging from the more rigid, whole class, teacher-oriented methods into a flexible, differentiated, pupil-oriented approach. One way to do this might be to start by considering various changes which could lead in the desired direction. Such changes might include:

- establishing a block of time for self-selected activities
- giving pupils a choice among assignments
- using self-correcting instructional materials
- giving pupils, individually and collectively, more voice in the selection of learning objectives.
- developing a constructive way of utilizing mistakes, errors and failures as a signal for the need to reevaluate and redirect effort
- scheduling more small group sessions
- initiating long-term, self-directing projects and activities
- providing opportunities for some one-to-one conferences with pupils
- initiating activities for the cooperative endeavor of pupil pairs or small pupil-teams
- utilizing more nonprint materials with small groups and individuals, as well as with the whole class.

Having listed a variety of possible changes, a second step would be to analyze these in terms of your readiness and that of your students. Which of the various choices seems to offer the easiest and most potentially successful changes you could initiate? Select two or three of these changes and concentrate your initial efforts on implementing them. You may wish to move gradually and unobtrusively into the new environment rather than catapulting yourself and your students into untried waters. Sending forth little feelers and taking short tentative steps makes any necessary retrenching and recouping easier to accomplish. You also have time to identify early those students who cannot easily handle too much freedom and adjust your plans accordingly. Two such approaches to the gradual opening up of the learning environment are described below. One relates to the establishment of a block of time for self-selection of activities. The other is centered around giving pupils a choice among assignments. Both are aimed at development of greater independence in students.

Providing Options for Self-Selection

This is an account of a second grade class whose teacher believed that even very young children can develop habits of self-direction in learning.

Each day for a two-week period, the teacher provided a short block of time in which children selected from specified activities the one which they would do. Generally, the time allotted was part of the "seatwork" time during reading group instruction. The alternatives from which the children could choose were limited, at first to two and later to three or four choices. The choices might be related, for example one day the children might be given a choice of two art activities—painting or clay modeling. On other days the activities were unrelated, such as choices between reading a library book, working with magnets or doing a "fun" math puzzle. At the end of each day's activity period, the children discussed the activity each had chosen, reasons for the choice and reactions to the activity.

During this two-week period three things had happened. First, the children had, in a limited way, engaged in self-selection of activities. Secondly, they had been exposed to and explored a wide variety of types of nonteacher-directed activities. And, finally, they had examined, through informal discussion, the decision-making process involved in self-selection. The teacher had also done several things. In keeping a daily record of each child's choice of activity, she had valuable feedback about the kinds of activities which were most popular, easiest for children to do without guidance, least conducive to disruptive problems, etc. She was able to identify those children who worked comfortably without teacher direction and those who would need more support and encouragement in learning to rely on their own judgment. She was also able to "field test" various spatial arrangements and identify problems related to storage and availability of materials and supplies which would need to be solved.

At the end of the two-week exploratory period, a list of all the activity alternatives was prepared. Each activity was entered on the list in words and by a picture symbol. A copy of the list was given to each child and a brief discussion about the activities held for the purpose of recalling all of them to mind. Children were then asked to go through the list and check any activity they would like to again be able to do. Children also discussed other possible choices, some of which were added to the lists. Each list was stapled to the outside of a large manila envelope with the child's name printed on it. The envelopes were kept in a box on the counter and were used to hold those completed or partly completed activities which would fit into them. The lists on the outside of each envelope served as reminders of the many activities from which a child might choose.

During subsequent weeks, increasingly larger amounts of time were made available for these self-selected activities. Some activities were always among the choices to be made. Others were offered on a kind of revolving schedule, while still others were of a "one time only" variety. New activities were gradually added until the options were quite extensive. The children's ability to select and independently pursue activities increased. Even those youngsters who at first had felt the need for the reassurance that it was "all right" to do so-and-so, soon became independent of this kind of support. Frequently, throughout the balance of the year, this class would set aside a whole afternoon for an Activity Fair. Regular choices for activities were available along with special extras, such as scheduled movies, playground time (supervised by volunteer mothers), story hour, a puppet theater presentation, a special type of art lesson, refreshments or "invite a friend to visit."

This teacher's venture into providing more freedom in the classroom was most successful. Occasionally, an activity would prove to be inappropriate. When this happened, the activity was simply withdrawn from the array of options. Other classroom routines and procedures continued as before and no great adjustment period was felt by teacher or children. Greater freedom just seemed to evolve naturally, with a minimum of effort and confusion.

Task Alternatives

A desire to give students an opportunity to choose from among alternative assignments led one sixth-grade teacher to modify his usual approach to homework requirements in math. These modifications did not at first venture very far from teacher-centered, whole class methodology, but the moves were very definitely in the direction of greater freedom and more opportunity for independence.

He made his first changes in the area of daily math assignments. Initially, the only alternatives open to students were the selection of "any ten examples on page 197 and any three problems on page 204." Or the assignment might be for everyone to "solve the following" and then select any one of three related activities. Soon the teacher provided more varied options. For example during a review of multiplication and division of fractions and mixed numbers, the choice could be between an assignment from the math textbook and a project involving the conversion of a casserole recipe for eight people into a recipe for 30, for 100 or for all 637 students in the school.

Later the teacher expanded the notion of choice of assignments to longer term tasks. For this he identified a learning objective and gave the students various alternative methods of pursuing the objective. Several different textbooks were made available as references, and appropriate page numbers for each were posted on a bulletin board. Daily teacher-led lessons were held for those students who wished to attend, and certain times each day were set aside for individual conferences. Students could work in pairs or alone, could use the textbooks or the daily lessons and conferences or they could combine all approaches. Several self-check tests were available for students to use when they felt they had mastered the objective. When a student was able to achieve a 90% or better score on two consecutive self-check tests, he was eligible to take the teacher-administered mastery test. As students completed the work for a given objective, they were directed to various review and maintenance activities or to several enrichment options, according to individual need. When a significant number of students was ready to go on, another learning objective was introduced and work continued in the same manner.

In each of the two illustrations just cited, the teacher concentrated on one modest change and made gradual moves toward freeing up the learning environment. There were no sudden disruptions of regular classroom routines, and both students and teachers emerged gently into the more open atmosphere. Since there is no one way which will surely meet the needs and styles of all children, it is not to be expected that all students will profit from the lifting of teacher-dominated instructional strategies. You will undoubtedly find one or two youngsters who will need considerable teacher direction. Likewise, there will very likely be several students in your class who could benefit from ever greater freedom. Thus, amount of teacher direction and control becomes another of the many ways in which you can differentiate your instructional programs.

GROUPING, SCHEDULING AND PLANNING

Other factors contributing to the intangible atmosphere in the classroom include grouping children, scheduling the day and planning activities. These factors can be manipulated to help create a growth-fostering environment or they can be used to build a rigid, confining cage. Consider for a moment the following account of a day in an elementary classroom.

9:00   *Opening Exercises:* Flag salute, attendance, lunch count, collections and announcements.

9:10   *Show-and-Tell:* Third row's turn today.

9:20   Explain morning's seatwork assignments.

9:30   *Reading*

	Group I	*Group II*	*Group III*
9:30– 10:00	Lesson: Story pp. 124 + . Develop vocabulary. Read & discuss pp. 124-28.	Seatwork	Workbook, pp. 27-29
10:00– 10:30	Workbook: pp. 74-75.	Lesson: Story pp. 153 + vc/cv syllabication. Read & discuss pp. 153-59.	Seatwork
10:30– 11:00	Seatwork	Workbook: pp. 90-91.	Lesson: Story pp. 81 + go over workbook. Read & discuss pp. 81-87.

11:00   Recess or game.

11:20   *Spelling* and *Handwriting*
       Spelling: p. 34
       Handwriting: review *a, c, d, g*

11:45   Lunch

12:15   Story Time

12:30   *Mathematics:* pp. 78-79. Do p. 78 together for practice. Assign p. 79. Work period.

1:20   Physical Education

2:00   *Science:* Filmstrip on "sound"

2:20   *Social Studies* and *English*
       Social Studies: pp. 104-110. Read and discuss.
       English: Write a page for the diary of an imaginary visitor to the New Amsterdam colony.

3:00   Dismissal

There is nothing unusual about this kind of daily planning. Entries similar to this can be found in planbooks in school districts across the country. What does it tell us about the way this teacher works with children? Except for reading, she works mostly with whole class groups. The material to be learned by the students appears to depend largely on what comes on the next pages in the textbook. Individual assistance may be given during the work period portion of math and possibly during the various language arts activities. Time is divided into blocks ranging from ten minutes to an hour. The specific activity to be engaged in during each block of time is predetermined, probably by the teacher. Except for the variations found between reading groups, all children perform the same activity at the same time.

What steps could this teacher take to loosen up these aspects of the learning environment? As with the physical aspects of environment, flexibility and organization are vital considerations. Flexibility and organization in grouping children and planning for daily activities call for considerable knowledge about each child. A teacher adhering to a schedule such as the one outlined above can "teach" all day without knowing very much about the students, because, in most cases, the textbook determines the lesson. But the teacher attempting to differentiate the learning program according to the needs, interests and styles of the individual children, has gathered much information about each child. This information guides the organization and requires the flexibility which is so essential to this teacher in her move toward a less rigid framework for learning.

Perhaps the first step for our teacher is in the realm of her own thinking about the teaching-learning process and the various roles of teacher and student. It might be wise for her to examine her reactions to ideas such as the following:

● My students can learn even when I am not telling them, working with them or watching them.

● Each child can learn something, although not all will learn the same thing or in the same time.

● Each child wants to progress, to find out, to do and to feel successful in learning.

● Every student has some characteristics which can be capitalized upon in the learning process.

● I have my own strengths and weaknesses to consider and must set realistic goals for instructional changes in my classroom. I do not have to be or teach just like Mrs. ＿＿＿ in order to be doing a good job.

● It is not necessary for me to work directly with each child in each subject every day.

● It is not essential for every child to work in every subject every day.

● There is nothing inherent in time, in any subject or in children which demands that blocks of time must be set aside when all children will work in a given subject area.

● An instructional group is valid only when each child in the group is likely to benefit from the activity. When the nature of the activity changes, the composition of the group will almost certainly need to be changed.

● Schedules and plans are suggested guidelines not regimented requirements for teacher or student.

When the teacher is able to agree with most of these ideas, she is ready to take further steps toward extending the potential of the learning environment. In the area of grouping, these steps may take form in short-term, specific skill groups, subdivision of the whole class into three or four subgroups for a particular subject (such as spelling) or small interest groups to pursue interdisciplinary projects. Specific examples of each of these types of grouping are given in subsequent chapters. A few guidelines for grouping practices can assist in deciding how to select group members for various occasions. The key factor is, of course, the purpose for which the group is assembled. Work in specific skills such as the short *a* vowel sound, addition of unlike fractions, use of quotation marks in writing or changing endings of base words before adding suffixes, is best done with small groups of students who are alike in their need for and readiness for the specific work to be developed. Heterogeneity is desirable for inquiry, experimentation, discussion, project work and other types of open-ended activity. Perhaps one of the best methods of grouping children for learning is to let children group themselves whenever possible. Knowing when to terminate an instructional group is equally as important as the wise selection of group members. Once the original goal for which the group was assembled has been met, the group should cease. Subsequent goals may result in new groups being formed with certain repetitions in membership, but group membership should be reviewed for each new purpose or goal.

Steps can also be taken to open up the scheduling and planning aspects of the learning environment. Larger blocks of interdisciplinary time can be scheduled during which a variety of small group activities can take place simultaneously. Some of these activities may involve teacher-led lessons for one group, teacher-specified activities for certain individuals and groups and self-selected projects and investigations for still other youngsters. Time can also be subdivided according to the type of activity rather than the subject to be studied. For example, one portion of each day may be set aside as a time for independent, quiet study and teacher-led small group instruction. One second grade class called this the "tiptoe and whisper" time of day. The use of contracts, job sheets and self-pacing instructional materials makes it possible to adopt a pick-up-tomorrow-where-you-left-off-today approach to planning. Greater student involvement in the planning of his own sequence and timing for a day's activity is enhanced by just such openendedness in the teacher's scheduling and planning.

One model for openness in scheduling and planning is the *divided day* plan. In this plan, the school day is divided into two roughly equal blocks of time. One time block, usually the morning period, is devoted to work in reading, math and language arts. During this period, children meet with the teacher individually or in small groups for conferences or instruction. Independent, self-directing and self-correcting activities supplement teacher-directed work. The afternoon, or second time block, is given over to self-selected activities at various learning and interest centers. This time may be spent in more work in the three R's or may be devoted to other kinds of endeavors such as science investigations, art, music or physical education activities, work in map exercises, community projects, drama, woodworking, etc. Each child decides what he would like to do and signs up for that activity for part or all of the time block. Certain activity centers are limited to a given number of participants and may be available on a first come, first served basis. This type of divided day plan has worked successfully with children from preschool age through sixth grade.

In some school systems, the plan has been followed by single teachers in self-contained classrooms and by small groups of teachers in several regular and/or double classrooms. In at least one urban school, the plan has enjoyed several years of successful growth and development throughout the entire school. Here classrooms are used as "home" rooms in the morning for skills instruction and become various activity centers during the afternoon. You can adapt the divided day plan to whatever system you are in. Even in a departmentalized organization, you can devote alternate days to teacher-directed sessions and self-selected activities.

Daily planning for a divided day will not look much like the planbook schedule outlined earlier in this discussion. Written plans become more horizontal, even three-dimensional, as the schedule

becomes more open. One section of a day's plans for the morning
might include these entries.

Small Group Sessions

Initial and final consonant substitution:
Mary, Tom, Alan, Debbie C., Phil
Long vowel sound with final silent *e:*
Bill V., Danny, Anne, Sophia,
John T., John M., Larry, Carole
Transition from manipulatives to vertical written algorism
for subtraction with regrouping of ones and tens:
Tom, Debbie C., Maria, Jane, Tony

Another section indicating activities to take place at the same time as
the small group sessions might look like this:

Listening Center   R *Language Master*

Multiplication drill record: Vocabulary practice:
Gary, Peter, Steven, Cathy   Terri
Consonant digraph tape: Paula
Susan, Betty Ann, Joanne   Anyone else interested
Spelling mastery test, lessons 16-20:
All level 2 group

Viewing Station—voluntary

filmstrips: Hansel and Gretel, The Ugly Duckling

A third section may be devoted to plans for individual conferences.

Conferences

Jeanne: general progress re: job sheet
check special geometry project
Bobby: reading conference
check for oral reading, especially better phrasing
and fewer repetitions
Francis: reading conference
give vocabulary recognition check tests
Sammy: plan new job sheet—
consider level C, Drawing Conclusions
start Paragraph Writing, set 2
continue practice in subtraction and include
project cards in measurement.

Any special activities to be engaged in by all children or by specific
youngsters might be listed in another section.

Specials: Whole Class
    11:30 Puppet show (Mrs. Carter's class visiting)
Specials: Testing
    Multiplication Mastery Test 4: Carole, Bobby,
        Ron
    Punctuation Diagnostic: John M.

All children will spend at least part of the morning period engaged in independent and self-directing activities. These do not appear in written daily plans, but are designated by job sheets, contracts or other long term assignments. Not all children will meet with the teacher on any given day. Frequency and length of direct contact with the teacher will vary according to need.

Summary

As soon as the physical classroom setting is peopled with teacher and students, we must consider the ways in which that teacher works with those children. The psychological climate in which the learning activities take place depends upon the teacher's concept of herself and her feelings toward her students. The teacher who values individuality and trusts her students, who provides opportunities for self-direction and inquiry and who fulfills a role of supportive guidance, will be likely to create a growth-fostering classroom environment. Effective ways of working with students also involve consideration of such concerns as scheduling time, planning activities and grouping children for instruction. Variety in grouping patterns based on the purpose of the activity; provision for self-selection of activities and for activities of an ongoing nature and establishment of larger blocks of interdisciplinary time such as in the divided day, are factors contributing to organization and flexibility in these important aspects of working with children in an atmosphere conducive to learning.

How to Go Beyond
Three Groups in Your
Reading Program

6

Reading is perhaps the most highly differentiated area of instruction currently found in our elementary schools. Common practice calls for subdividing a class into three smaller groups according to level. Children are usually placed in a group on the basis of a score earned on an achievement or diagnostic test or because they have completed work in a basal reading series up to such-and-such a point. The teacher generally meets with each group daily for a teacher-led lesson and provides each group with follow-up activities to be worked on independently while she meets with the other two groups. Flexibility is likely to involve occasionally moving a youngster to a higher or lower group. As a first step in differentiating the reading program, the three-group plan can be of value. If differentiation is limited to this approach, its value is also limited.

Another approach to providing for differences in reading abilities is the "homogeneous" grouping of children for classroom assignments. Children of similar reading levels are assigned to a given teacher either on an all day, all year basis or for a daily block of time designated for reading instruction. Many so-called nongraded plans use this "levels" approach to class composition. There are many reasons, in addition to those related to reading instruction, for considering this plan of questionable desirability for elementary school children.

One of the greatest dangers in the three-group plan or the homogeneous levels plan is the tendency of many teachers to operate on the assumption that because these ten or these 30 children are "all at the same level" in reading, they can be instructed as a single entity. Even when the 30 homogeneously assigned children are subdivided into two or three smaller groups, any one of these subgroups cannot effectively be handled as a single whole. Another danger in assigning children to reading groups or classes on the basis of reading level is the tendency of many teachers to lock-step all children in the group into a pattern of going through the book, story by story, and through the workbook, page by page. Such a system is not only deadly in its monotony, but also it is inefficient in its assumption that all these children need or are ready for every lesson sequenced into the program.

Let us consider the case of two fourth grade students who would be placed together in a group on the basis of their score on the Bond, Bolow, Hoyt New Developmental Reading Tests*. Both of these students were considered advanced readers and achieved a grade level equivalency score of 6.5. This score represents the average of the comprehension subtest scores. A separate score for basic reading vocabulary is also provided by this diagnostic test. The graph in Figure 6-1 shows a breakdown of the comprehension subtest scores and includes the vocabulary recognition score.

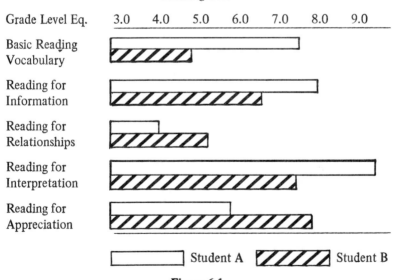

Scores Earned by Two Fourth Grade Students on the Bond, Bolow, Hoyt New Developmental Reading Test

Figure 6-1

An analysis of this profile shows that, while both students achieved an average score of 6.5, there the similarity ends. Vocabulary recognition scores show a difference of 3.0 grade levels. Differences

*Lyons and Carnahan, Inc.

in comprehension subskill areas range from 1.0 grade levels in Reading for Relationships to 2.2 grade levels in Reading for Appreciation. Student *A* could use some practice in Reading for Appreciation, but this would be virtually a waste of time for Student *B* who might better concentrate his efforts on vocabulary building. If two so-called homogeneously grouped advanced readers with identical average scores show this kind of heterogeneity, consider the picture you would derive for ten or more students whose *average* scores are merely similar, perhaps within a one-year range. And this test is limited to a few comprehension aspects of reading, giving no analysis of word attack subskills.

Since it appears quite obvious that even in small reading groups, meaningful homogeneity is a myth, the need for greater differentiation within or beyond the reading group becomes apparent. What can the classroom teacher do to overcome the limitations of the three-group approach without creating insurmountable scheduling and organizational problems? This chapter discusses two teachers' plans for differentiating reading instruction. One teacher started with the three-group plan and found three avenues for providing greater individualization within this framework. The second teacher abandoned the three-group plan and developed a semi-individualized program based on a diagnostic-prescriptive format for continuous progress.

BRANCHING OUT

Mrs. Richardson started September with 28 students. Reading record cards showed that 12 of her students were ready to begin the first second grade basal, ten fell below this level and six were above it. On the basis of this information, she established three reading groups. The youngsters in the lowest group (Group I) ranged from preprimer to first reader level; those in the highest group (Group III) ranged up to high third grade level. Mrs. Richardson felt that the need for differentiation was most pressing for Group I. This would also be the most difficult to achieve since these children needed the greatest amount of teacher direction and had developed virtually no independent work habits.

Using Pupil-Teams in the Reading Group

For her first step, Mrs. Richardson decided to pair the children in Group I in pupil teams as homogeneously as possible on the basis of recognition of vocabulary words. To do this, she prepared a list of vocabulary words taken from the basal reader used in her school. Her list included all words from the preprimers and primer and most of the words from the first reader. She tested each child individually on his ability to orally read the listed words. On the basis of this information, Mrs. Richardson paired the children according to rank order. She also used results of the test to prepare individual lists of words for each child to learn as sight words, and to prepare a set of flash cards for each child. To do this she printed one word on both sides of a flash card. The set of cards prepared for each child contained ten known and five unknown words. The child was then asked to draw on one side of each unknown word card a picture which would help him remember that word. Next, Mrs. Richardson worked with these ten children to show them how to study the flash cards both independently and with a partner. A child from Group III was designated as resource person for each team. As a child mastered his new words (knew them perfectly in oral recognition checks on three separate days), five of the original known words were eliminated from the set and five new unknown words were added. In this way the child was always sufficiently challenged with new words to learn, but not overwhelmed by the task. Mrs. Richardson felt that including two known words for every unknown word provided a satisfying degree of success during every practice session. Periodic review of all words kept the child exposed to them and also made him aware of the progress he was making.

In addition to work with flash cards, Mrs. Richardson provided a variety of prereading and beginning reading activities which these children could do alone, with their partners or in groups of four. Some of these activities involved the use of manipulatives—objects, pictures, word cards, etc.—which were to be matched, sorted or put in order according to some specified criterion. Others were game or puzzle type activities including commercially available ones, as well as items which Mrs. Richardson designed and made herself. Paper-and-pencil type activities were also included and answer keys utilized whenever possible. Mrs. Richardson was thus able to provide differentiated "seatwork" assignments for Group I students and also provided an opportunity each day for self-selection of some reading activities.

Expanding the use of pupil-teams to the remaining two reading groups was the next step. Group II seemed to be the best group to work with using a conventional teacher-led group lesson. Therefore, Mrs. Richardson introduced the pupil-team approach next to Group III. Reading record cards indicated that in this group, two children had started the 2-2 basal, two others had completed the 2-2 basal, one was about halfway through the 3-1 book and the sixth child had been reading independently in an "enrichment" program. Mrs. Richardson individually administered informal reading inventories to these six students. She found that the 2-2 level was a comfortable and appropriate one for the first two youngsters in the group. The other four did not fall neatly into pairs according to general level. Based on the informal inventory results, instructional levels for these four children were approximately 3-1, 3-2, 4-1 and 5 or better. Mrs. Richardson decided to pair the two 2-2 children as a team and to have them continue working in the 2-2 basal program. The other four were paired on the basis of compatibility and would use self-selected trade books for the silent and oral reading aspects of their programs.

Job sheets were designed to guide the activities of these three pupil-teams. For the 2-2 team, the job sheet centered around stories, workbook exercises and other related activities suggested by the basal program with considerable opportunity to extend reading to self-selected books and stories from other readers. Job sheets designed for the remaining two teams provided greater latitude for self-direction since they merely provided suggestions and guidelines rather than specific assignments. Excerpts from samples of these two kinds of job sheets are shown in Figures 6-2 and 6-3.

***Lippincott's Basic Reading
Book F: Job Sheet
Part 3: Fun with Animals**

Put a check in each box when you have finished that job.

TITLE	TEXT PAGES	WKBK PAGES	Do at Least One of the Choices for Each Story
☐ A Strange Friend	☐ 96-100 ☐ 100-108	☐ 30, 32 ☐ 33-35	☐ Workbook p. 31. ☐ Find a poem about deer and/or other wild animals. Copy it for our poetry book.

Figure 6-2

*J.B. Lippincott Company

TITLE	TEXT PAGES	WKBK PAGES	Do at Least One of the Choices for Each Story
	☐109-114	☐36-39	☐Draw a "filmstrip" about the story.
☐Henry and Ribs	☐115-119	☐40-42	☐Find a library book by Beverly Cleary. ☐Read some of it orally with your partner.
	☐120-131	☐43-46	☐Draw a picture to go with p. 124 in Book F.
	☐132-140	☐47-49	☐Write a paragraph telling about a dog you know.
☐The Hairy Dog	☐141	☐50-51	☐Write a list of at least five kinds (breeds) of dogs who have hair covering their eyes.
☐The Night Rain	☐142	☐52	☐Write or copy a poem about rain for our poetry book. ☐Draw a picture showing some things children can do inside on a rainy day.

Other Activities: Do at least two of these.

☐ Read and write a report for any book by Beverly Cleary, or any book about a dog, or any book about a deer.

☐ Make a poetry booklet about weather or about animals. Write or copy several poems—only one poem on each page. Make drawings around or near the poem.

☐ Draw and write a comic strip story about an animal.

☐ Make an exhibit about some kind of wild animal. Be sure to show us about his home, his food, his protection from enemies and what he looks like.

Figure 6-2 (Continued)

Job Sheet for Independent Reading

Topic III: *Interesting People*

   A. Select and read at least two books about interesting people—
      either real or make-believe.

   B. For each book do the following things.

      1. On a 5-by-8 index card write the title of the book, the author's
         name, a few sentences about the book, your name and your
         opinion about the book.

      2. In your vocabulary notebook, list important or interesting
         new words you found in the book. Give the meaning of each
         or use it in a sentence *or* illustrate it with a drawing.

      3. Select a section or chapter of the book to share with your
         partner and read it aloud to him.

   C. Choose one of the books you have read and make a mural, a
      diorama or some other visual about the person.

Figure 6-3

The last group to be introduced to pupil-teaming was Group II. For the members of this group, composition of the pupil-teams was based primarily on skill in auditory discrimination. Mrs. Richardson used the phonics portion of the Botel Reading Inventory* to assess these skills, and children were paired on the basis of their position on the auditory identification continuum shown below.

| Initial Consonant Sounds | → | Initial Consonant Blends | → | Consonant Digraphs | → | Long Vowel Sounds | → | Short Vowel Sounds | → | Other Vowel Sounds |

The children in this group would spend the "seatwork" portion of a reading period partly in working with the partner on specified activities and partly in working on self-selected reading activities. Most specified activities were listed in a study guide which all teams in the group would do. Some other specified activities were especially assigned to a team by the teacher to reinforce and extend specific reading subskills. An example of a study guide used by all teams in Group II is shown in Figure 6-4. Answer columns were covered while children answered a set of questions, then uncovered to allow them to check their work before going onto the next section.

---

*Follett Publishing Company

*Lippincott's Basic Reading
Book E: Study Guide

Kit Carson—Famous Hunter

A   pp. 209–210

1. when he was a
   small boy
2. to find out
   what kind of
   lands were in
   the West
3. he kept on go-
   ing to the
   West
4. strong, brave,
   calm, honest

1. When did Kit Carson know he wanted to
   be a hunter and trapper?
2. Why did Kit and the other men go west?

3. What did Kit do when the other men
   turned back in New Mexico?

4. Reread the last paragraph on page 210.
   Find four words that tell what kind of man
   Kit Carson was.

B   pp. 211–214

5. large, dan-
   gerous, smart
6. he hit them on
   the nose with a
   stick when they
   started to
   climb up
7. all night

8. he threw
   crumbs down
   for them to
   eat

5. What words will tell about the grizzly bear?

6. How did Kit Carson keep the bears from
   coming up the tree to get him?

7. How long did the bears keep him up the
   tree?
8. How did Kit get the bears to go away?

C   pp. 215–217

9. the wolves
   had eaten it
   during the
   night
10.   5
        2
        3

9. Why didn't Kit Carson take the deer he
   had shot back to camp with him?

10. Put these sentences in the right order so
    they tell what happened to Kit after his
    night in the tree.

Figure 6-4

*J.B. Lippincott Company

Kit Carson—Famous Hunter

C   pp. 215–217 (Cont'd.)

4   __He told the folks about what had
1   happened
                         __He walked back to camp
                         __He ate a meal of deer meat
                         __He took a short rest
                         __He climbed down from the tree

D   Find and write the word that means each of
     these:

11. wilderness	11. p. 209 wild place
12. calm	12. p. 210 unexcited
13. huge	13. p. 211 very large
14. gnarled	14. p. 212 twisted, knotted
15. gnawed	15. p. 213 bit at and wore away
16. rap, rapped	16. p. 214 hit
17. numb	17. p. 215 not able to feel or move
18. folks	18. p. 216 people
19. mighty	19. p. 217 great, important

E   Read orally with your partner pp. 211-214

20. gnarled,   20. Find all the words in this part of the story
    gnawed,   which have the "n" sound for "gn". Write
    gnashed   them.

Figure 6-4 (Continued)

Any workbooks, worksheets or duplicated exercises to be used by teams in the basal readers would be assigned one copy per team. Answers were to be agreed upon by the team, and only one response recorded for the partnership except in cases of disagreements which could not be resolved by discussion. Then both answers would be entered on the same page and initialed by the appropriate pupil. In most cases, teachers' editions or answer keys were provided to make the activities self-correcting.

Varying the Amount of Teacher Direction

In addition to the use of pupil-teams within reading groups, Mrs. Richardson found other avenues for differentiating instruction. One of these involved varying the frequency and extent of teacher direction and contact. Different teams within a reading group would need different amounts of teacher guidance. Certain teams seemed to require more extensive work in vocabulary development, other teams needed additional assistance in comprehension and interpretation of material read, still other teams benefited from greater guidance in following study guides or in budgeting time during independent work periods.

The frequency and duration of teacher-led group sessions varied from group to group. Mrs. Richardson found it necessary to meet briefly with Group I at the beginning of each day's reading time block. This time was generally devoted to helping the pupil-teams get organized and underway with the day's specific reading activities. In addition to this, she spent time each day in teacher-led reading activities with every child in this group. Sometimes the activity would involve all members of the group. At other times, Mrs. Richardson would meet with one or two teams at a time until all children in the group had worked with her in at least one subgroup session every day. The subgroup sessions were necessarily brief and almost always were followed by provision for individual or small group involvement in an activity related to the day's "lesson."

Different plans emerged for the other two groups. Mrs. Richardson generally met the entire Group II for a teacher-directed lesson about twice a week. The other three days were devoted to subgroup sessions dealing with specific reading skills and team conferences. On any one day, Mrs. Richardson might hold from one to three skills sessions and three or more team conferences. A given Group II child might attend all possible skill sessions in a week, or he might attend none, depending upon the teacher's assessment of his need for those particular lessons. Group III youngsters needed much less teacher guidance. Teacher contact here generally took the form of weekly team conferences with occasional whole-group get-togethers for a lesson or discussion.

The team conference situation for members of Group II provided another means for differentiating both the amount and type of teacher contact and direction. Some pupil-teams seemed to need two or even three conferences a week while most teams managed very well with only one. A typical conference would begin with a discussion and assessment of progress, with study guides, assignments and self-selected activities pursued since the last conference. Each child would read orally one or two pages which he had selected from one of the stories read recently. Mrs. Richardson would then make suggestions for improving word attack or comprehension skills, introduce specific assignments, provide for further discussion or encourage pupil self-evaluation according to the apparent needs of the pupils involved.

Providing for Self-Selection of Independent Activities

A third avenue for differentiation in reading was found in the provision of opportunities for pupils to choose those independent activities which appealed to them. If such opportunities are to exist, it is necessary for a wide variety of materials and activities to be available and readily accessible. Children must have the time and the know-how for using these materials and they must feel at liberty to select any activity they wish—even if it seems by adult standards to be too easy, too difficult or too much of the same thing.

A child who is having a struggle in learning some new skill or concept may, when given an opportunity to choose his own activity, select a very easy one simply to take the pressure off himself for awhile. On the other hand, a very lively interest in a topic or type of activity may lead some children to choose material that is generally too difficult. If the activity proves to be of no value to him the youngster will soon abandon it for something else. Children's interests, like that of adults, often run in streaks. You can probably recall occasions when you had a "run on" some activity, playing golf or bridge or reading mystery stories. It is not unnatural for children to experience such periods when they are especially interested in just one or two of the activities made available for self-selection. If a child seems always to choose to read horse stories, to look at dinosaur pictures or to play the same word game, rest assured that he is finding some personal value in the repeated activity. The value may be social (he enjoys doing things with Steve) or personal (he gets a feeling of confidence from continuing success experiences) rather than primarily academic, but the value is real and important to him. If it were not, he would naturally select some other activity which would be more appropriate for his needs.

Mrs. Richardson found that three basic types of activities provided a good range of selections for her class. The first of these was a "library" of things to read, look at or listen to. A wide variety of books, magazines, catalogs, records and tapes was selected to accommodate the various levels and interests in the classroom. Changes and additions were made from time to time to keep the collection intriguing. Suggestions for projects and materials for carrying them out served as the basis for a second type of activity. Puppet theater supplies and a box of props and costumes encouraged dramatizations. Tapes were available for recording stories or poems. Art supplies could be used to make charts, bulletin boards, dioramas or pictures about stories a child had read or written. The third group of activities included a collection of games and game-like materials. In addition to commercially available reading and word building games, Mrs. Richardson provided an assortment of teacher-made activities. Some of these were reading readiness items such as design cards to match for visual discrimination. Simple reading tasks were modified to a game format. For example, vocabulary words were printed on a tic-tac-toe game board for practice in word recognition. Even old seatwork worksheets were placed in a Hodge Podge Box for children to do "just for fun," and many children will tell you it's lots more fun to do worksheets when you don't really *have* to do them. Figures 6-5 and 6-6 give examples of design cards and vocabulary tic-tac-toe.

DESIGN CARD TO MATCH
FOR VISUAL DISCRIMINATION

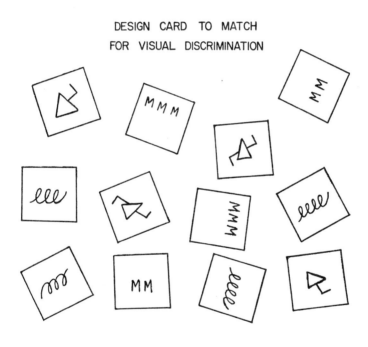

Figure 6-5

Each of the avenues Mrs. Richardson utilized made it possible for her to increase the amount of differentiation in her reading program without abandoning the three-group framework. The use of pupil-teams provided a means for allowing children within a reading group to progress at different rates and levels and to concentrate on specific skills as needed. Varying the amount of time which children spent in teacher-led sessions enabled Mrs. Richardson to gear both the quantity and the type of teacher instruction to the needs of specific children. Availability of many materials for student self-

Game Boards for Vocabulary TIC-TAC-TOE

two	some	play	find	four	ride
down	this	funny	told	was	o'clock
come	house	upon	swing	yellow	best

looked	quick	first	rode	orange	your
picture	them	elephant	store	here	smiling
brown	sailing	write	today	seven	maybe

In playing Vocabulary TIC-TAC-TOE, a youngster must point to the space where he wishes to place his marker and read the word correctly before he may put his marker on the board. If he does not read the word correctly, he loses his turn. Colored blocks are used instead of X's and O's. Four sets of TIC-TAC-TOE can be played on each game board. Game boards are printed on oaktag and protected by acetate covers.

Figure 6-6

selection provided even greater possibilities for differentiation of independent activities. Taken all together and combined with those more conventional practices which she retained, these techniques added up to a very vital and effective reading program.

INDIVIDUALIZING A READING PROGRAM

When teachers talk about individualized reading, it is unlikely that they all mean the same thing by the term. Concepts about what constitutes individualized reading vary greatly from school to school and from teacher to teacher.

To some teachers, the fact that a child is moving through an established developmental reading program "at his own rate" reading the stories and doing the workbook pages by himself with periodic checks by the teacher—is enough to call the approach individualized. Here individualization is equated with working independently and at a personalized rate. All children in this kind of plan will be expected to work through essentially the same program, the main provision for differentiation being timing—the *when* and *how fast* aspects of instruction. Some provision may also be made for extra help and extra practice in specific skills which cause difficulty for a given child. This type of plan is often found in so-called nongraded schools where grade level labels have been replaced with reading level classifications or tracks based upon a basal or other developmental reading program.

A second model for individualized reading might be referred to as the Self-Selection/Conference Plan. In this approach the child chooses his own reading material, generally from a classroom library. The teacher assesses the child's progress through the medium of the pupil-teacher conference commonly held on a weekly basis. During these conferences, specific instruction may be given according to the teacher's determination of the child's need. Follow-up assignments may also be given to provide practice in the new skill or concept. The self-selection/conference plan for individualized reading assumes a high degree of sophistication in the teacher's familiarity with developmental reading skills and her ability to assess the child's needs during the course of the weekly conference. Many teachers have the expertise requisite for administering such a program. Others do not. If you feel you fall into this latter category, perhaps a more highly structured model would serve your purposes to greater advantage.

The diagnostic-prescriptive model is just such a structured approach to individualized reading. Programs fashioned on this model are based on the premise that reading can be broken down into many small skills which are arranged in some sort of sequence or matrix. Each skill is generally stated in the form of pupil behavior which can be measured objectively. Tests or tasks provide a means for this measurement of the child's ability to perform the particular skill to a specified degree of satisfaction. This process is the diagnostic aspect of the program. Its purpose is to assist the teacher in identifying those children who have mastered a given skill and those children who need instruction in that skill. The prescriptive aspect of the program suggests activities and materials for the child to work on for the purpose of mastering the skill. Some programs provide these activities and materials, others itemize them and tell where they may be obtained. A second test or evaluation task measures the degree of success a child has had in mastering the objective as a result of following the prescribed instructional activities.

Instructional management and monitoring programs are based on the diagnostic-prescriptive model. One such program provides the evaluation instruments and itemizes specific portions of readily available self-directing, self-correcting instructional materials for the prescriptive aspect of each of hundreds of reading skills. Another provides evaluation instruments and itemizes specific portions of several major developmental reading programs which can be utilized for prescribing instructional activities for each of the reading skills identified in the program. Both systems provide for flexibility in sequencing a child's progress in the program.

Arguments pro and con can be advanced for each of the three models described above. The independently pursued basal program is perhaps the easiest to administer since it deviates least from most conventional group plans. It is also a realistic possibility for teachers who are obliged to use a given basal reader program because of school policy. This plan, however, offers the least flexibility and the least range for differentiation of any of the three models considered. The self-selection/conference plan, on the other hand, offers a great deal of flexibility and a wide range of opportunity for differentiation. Drawing upon the interests of the child to a very high degree, it can result in much enthusiasm on the part of students. This model has the disadvantage of providing a minimum amount of structure for the teacher (or student) who wants or needs this kind of support and guidance. Many teachers attempting this plan have found that the program soon flounders due to lack of direction. Direction, continuity and structure must be provided by the teacher. In the diagnostic-prescriptive approach, direction, continuity and structure are the strong points of the program. Here planning, testing and determining of instructional methods have all been worked out for the teacher. The teacher becomes to a large degree, merely an administrator of a program. Thus the program runs the danger of becoming automated, mechanical and impersonal.

The classroom teacher desiring to individualize her reading program is thus faced with the necessity of choosing a basic approach to this task. The three models considered here are by no means exhaustive but they are three very commonly utilized plans. How does a teacher determine which approach to use? Many teachers will find that a consideration of each plan will result in a fairly strong preference for one of them over the other two. The advantages of this one approach will appear more desirable or feasible for a particular teacher's style, her pupils or her teaching situation. Other teachers may wish to incorporate certain aspects from more than one model into a "best of both" program. A "best of both" approach was the one undertaken by Mr. Tuttle, a fourth grade teacher whose program development we shall now consider.

The unique advantages of the self-selection/conference plan and those of the diagnostic-prescriptive plan both appealed to Mr. Tuttle. Furthermore, he felt that the strengths of each tended to counterbalance the weaknesses of the other. At first glance, these approaches to individualized reading might appear to be at opposite ends of a continuum, and therefore incompatible. Mr. Tuttle decided to attempt the design of a program which would utilize what he felt to be the best practices in each program and incorporate them into a single, but double-faceted program. Underlying his program were two broad general goals:

1. Each child will develop greater enthusiasm for reading.
2. Each child will progress in word attack and comprehension skills.

Strategies for reaching the first of these goals were closely related to the self-selection/conference plan with a few modifications and techniques of his own added. Methods employed for the second goal resembled the diagnostic-prescriptive approach, although they were less elaborate than the programs described earlier in this chapter.

Developing Enthusiasm for Reading

Real enthusiasm for reading is a force which must be generated from within the child. Fancy motivational gimmicks and antics on the part of the teacher may momentarily entertain children, but they do little toward instilling a lasting excitement about books. Mr. Tuttle decided to let the children themselves serve as catalysts for getting the free reading aspect of his program under way. He felt that by providing plenty of books, ample time for unstructured reading and many opportunities for sharing the "good parts" of stories, he would help to establish an atmosphere conducive to the enjoyment of reading. The spark which would make the whole plan catch fire would need to come from the children.

With these general ideas in mind, Mr. Tuttle approached the first day of school with only five words entered in his planbook under the heading for Reading:

"Survey and discuss favorite books."

He asked the children to think back over all the various books they had ever read or that someone had read to them or which they had seen dramatized in movies or on television and to think of five which they thought were among their favorites. Each child was asked to list these five favorites by title, main character or some other identifying notation. At this point several children wished to talk about books they had read, and this was, of course, encouraged. For those who did not enter into this spontaneous discussion, an opportunity was provided to read aloud their lists of favorite books if they wished. Some children did not contribute orally to any part of the activity, but all turned in a list of books.

These lists became the basis of the classroom library. Every effort was made to obtain each book appearing on one of these lists. Occasionally it was necessary to ask a child to bring a book from home to lend to the library, but most were readily available through the school or public library. A few could not be obtained, and one or two could not be identified from the child's description. For many books listed, additional titles by the same authors were also included. Mr. Tuttle selected a dozen or so of his own favorites and the school librarian added quite a few volumes to round out the collection. To this were added paperbacks, cartoon and comic books and several children's and popular adult magazines, including some devoted to jokes and riddles. By the end of a week, over 200 books and magazines were available in the classroom library.

On the second day of school, when the classroom library was still in its infancy, a composite list of favorite books was distributed to each child. A question-and-answer period followed during which children who had read the book under discussion answered questions from other children, questions such as:

> What was this story about?
>
> Was that the one about the spider and the pig?
>
> Why did you think so-and-so was such a good story?
>
> I started to read it once and I thought it was stupid!

Favorite of the Favorites

As soon as the classroom library was well established, Mr. Tuttle announced a book contest. This contest would last all semester and the books, not the children, were to be the contestants. Any book in the classroom library could be nominated. Nominations were to be held one week later. Each child was encouraged to nominate his own favorite book to "run for" *Favorite of the Favorites.* No one was required to nominate a book and no one could nominate more than one book, although a given book could be nominated by more than one student. To nominate a book, the student was to give the title and author, hold the book up for everyone to see and give one of three kinds of nominating presentation designed to make others want to read the book.

1. Tell about the book, but don't give away any important secrets of the story.
2. Read a funny, exciting, spooky or otherwise interesting selection from the book (no more than three pages long).
3. Prepare (and explain) a visual exhibit about the book—a picture, shoebox diorama, etc.

In all, 16 books were nominated—three of them by two students and one by three students. Several children chose not to nominate any book. A list of the 16 nominees was posted near the classroom library and children were encouraged to include some of these among their selections for free reading. At the end of the semester, a vote was taken to elect the Favorite of the Favorites.

Desk Top Libraries

Each child was asked to maintain a desk top library which would consist of at least two and not more than four books and/or magazines from which he could select his reading material during the daily free reading time. At the beginning of this period, all desk top libraries would be placed on the desk tops for easy access. During the period, children were free to exchange books from their desk top libraries for new material from the classroom libraries. Lending from the desk top library to classmates was also permitted. Books and magazines from home or from the school or public libraries were included in the desk top libraries. When not in use during free reading time, these materials were kept in student desks or in designated sections of the storage shelves built in the classroom.

Mr. Tuttle believed that many lukewarm and reluctant readers are discouraged from reading in school because so much written work usually accompanies each reading selection. For this reason he did not require any written book reports and did not sponsor any reading contest of the usual sort, or keep any public record of the number of books read by each student. Only a brief record of books read was required, and this was done by the student himself and kept with his desk top library. This record consisted of a small spiral notebook in which the child kept track of each book he read—one book to a page. He was asked to include on this page the title of the book, the author's name, one or two words describing the type of book, such as *animal* or *sports* or *biography* and a numerical rating of from 1 to 4 expressing his opinion of the book. One was the lowest or poorest rating, 4 the highest. In addition to this required data, the child could add any information or comment he wished. Thus the free reading period became a time of reading for pleasure with a very minimum of required tasks or written work.

A Classroom Scrapbook

A second, strictly voluntary method of recording information about books was provided by the classroom scrapbook. Pages for the scrapbook were made from 12-by-18 sheets of manila paper with three holes punched along one side to receive large metal rings. To contribute to the scrapbook, a child printed the name of the author, directory style, at the top of a page. Under this he wrote the title of the book. He then added his contribution about the story and inserted the page in the scrapbook in alphabetical order by author's last name. Thereafter, any child could add more to the page until it was filled, when another page for that book could be started. Contributions could be in the form of comments about the story, book reports, quotations, lists of interesting words, pictures about events in the book, etc. Children were asked to prepare their contributions on smaller sheets of writing or drawing paper and then paste them on the scrapbook page. In this way, a partially filled page would not be spoiled if a child made a mistake and needed to copy his work on a new sheet of paper.

The classroom scrapbook provided an exhibit place for children who especially like to write reports or draw pictures about books. Children could sign their contributions or not, as they pleased. No one was *required* to contribute at any time. Certain patterns regarding the use of the scrapbook were observed. A few children contributed pictures quite regularly. One or two frequently wrote reports. One boy regularly contributed intricately labeled illustrations from science books he read. Two children often looked through the scrapbook but never added anything to it. A few never contributed and never looked at it, but most children went through alternating periods of using or ignoring the scrapbook. When other classroom projects were at a high pitch, the scrapbook was virtually forgotten for a short period of time until a spurt of renewed interest brought it back to life.

Post-Reading Activities

About three times each week, the free reading period would be abbreviated for 15-20 minutes to allow time for a group activity related to reading. Except on occasion, the children could opt to continue reading rather than joining the group activity. The purposes of the activities were to provide opportunities to share ideas about the books being read and to build-in some fun which might, in turn, stimulate enthusiasm for more reading.

An effort was made to vary the type of activity. Perhaps one day the time would be devoted to an informal kind of sharing when children could volunteer to give brief reports or oral readings, or when small groups would have "book talks" and serve Kool-Aid tea. At a book talk one child would review a particular book and others who had read the book might then comment. This would be followed by a question-and-answer period. Two or three book talk groups could meet simultaneously.

On another day the activity might be more game-like. Charades and pantomimes were popular. One guessing game frequently requested was called simply the "I'm thinking of" Game and was played according to a very familiar format. The child who was *It* would think of a title, a character or an event for one of the books in the classroom library. He would then give a clue.

"I'm thinking of a book in which . . ."

"I'm thinking of someone who . . ."

"I'm thinking of the time when . . ."

The child who guessed correctly became *It* and the game proceeded. A written form of the guessing game was also played occasionally. Children contributed clues for this game by writing each on a slip of paper with the answer on the back and depositing it in a sealed box on the teacher's desk. When enough clues had accumulated, they were compiled on a dittoed sheet. A specified amount of time was allowed for children to attempt answering all the clues. During this time, it was legal to refer to any books or to their own personal record of books read. When the time was up, correct answers were given and a tally made of total scores. Clues similar to those given in Figure 6-7 were typical. How many can you answer correctly? Answers are included in this sample illustration so you can check yourself. During the regular playing of the game, answers were given orally.

CAN YOU GUESS?

1. I am a story character. Usually I am sad and gloomy. One day I was surprised and very happy to get two very unusual birthday gifts. Who am I?_____

2. I am a book. I tell about a boy who tries to tell everyone about something important. But no one pays any attention to him for a long time. What is my title?_____

3. I am a book. I am easy and fun to read. The first part of me is about fish. To read me is sort of like reading poetry. What is my title?
_____

4. I am a story character but I am not a person or an animal. My name describes the sound I make. Because of me a family had many exciting adventures. My name is also the title of a book about me. Who am I?
_____

Answers:

1. Eeyore, the old gray donkey from *Winnie the Pooh* by A.A. Milne (Dutton)

2. *Nobody Listens to Andrew* by Elizabeth Guilfoile (Follett)

3. *One Fish, Two Fish, Red Fish, Blue Fish* by Dr. Seuss (Beginner Books)

4. Chitty Chitty Bang Bang. Book by Ian Fleming (Random House)

Figure 6-7

The third activity for a given week was likely to be of a special presentation nature. This might take the form of one of the following:

● A student production dramatizing events from one of the books.

● A mock TV interview with an author revealing interesting information about his life and the stories he had written.

● A filmstrip-tape or recorded presentation of a story.

● A special film such as *The Story of a Book* (Waterman Productions) which explains how the author conceived, wrote and illustrated a children's book about a hermit crab.*

● An extra trip to the school library to hear a new story read.

● A special introduction to the books of a particular author, such as the collection of delightfully illustrated books of Brian Wildsmith.**

● A session devoted to the planning of an exhibit, a bulletin board or a library display.

● An unveiling and exhibition of peep show boxes depicting stories read by the exhibitors. (A peep show is a small closed box, such as a shoe box with the cover on, containing a diorama. The viewer looks through a small peephole in one end of the box. Inconspicuous holes or slits in the box are needed to admit light.)

The Finishing Touches

To round out this aspect of Mr. Tuttle's reading program, he spotted several reading activities throughout the day. Mr. Tuttle was the main participant in some of these activities. For example, he set aside a short period of time each day during which he read aloud to the class. New books were frequently added to the classroom library by having him read aloud part of the book. As a rule, Mr. Tuttle read only one episode, section or chapter from a book—just enough to get children interested and wanting to read more on their own. Mr. Tuttle also made a practice of having on his own desk a book which he was reading for his own pleasure. Whenever spare moments allowed, when the children were taking a test or were having their free reading time, he would pick up his own book and read for awhile. Often he was able to share with the class a humorous or interesting passage from his book or discuss with them an intriguing idea suggested by it. In this way, Mr. Tuttle served as a model, deriving pleasure from his own reading and sharing it with others.

Pagoo by Holling C. Holling, Houghton-Mifflin.
**Franklin Watts, Inc.

Student participation in spontaneous small group activities during free reading period and at other times during the day was encouraged. Multiple copies of assorted basal readers and children's paperbacks were added to the classroom library. A class discussion was held to consider various ways in which these materials could be used. Several ideas emerged and remained popular throughout the year. One activity was called Read Aloud. It was simply two or three youngsters, each with a copy of a given book, taking turns to read the story aloud to each other and anyone else who wished to listen. Another favorite, called Read Along, was a kind of informal choral reading activity. Reading Marathons were a bit more competitive and appealed mostly to better-than-average readers. This activity called for one child in a small group to read aloud just as long as he could without making an error. As soon as he made an error it was another youngster's turn to continue with the story on the same basis. A very popular activity among the girls was playing school. One youngster would assume the role of teacher and conduct a "reading lesson" for the others in the group. Oral reading from a basal reader and exercises at the chalkboard constituted the bulk of this activity. Basal readers also served the class as a source of short stories for independent reading. Parallel silent reading was another favorite. For this activity two or three youngsters would congregate in some corner of the room to read silently but companionably, each from his own book. Occasionally, reading would be interrupted for a friendly chat just as it would if adults were sharing an evening of reading.

Spontaneous small group activities such as these provided a change of pace during the free reading period. Many children, especially those who have not generally found much pleasure in reading, often find it difficult to spend more than 20 or 25 minutes in independent silent reading. Since the free reading period lasted about twice as long as this, it was certainly desirable for them to have alternative activities from which to choose.

Making Progress in Reading Skills

The second major aspect of Mr. Tuttle's program dealt with the child's progress in word attack and comprehension skills. In preparing for this phase of instruction, Mr. Tuttle first identified his general objectives in the form of a checklist of skills. The items on this list were drawn from scope and sequence charts of several basal reading programs. Each skill was then analyzed and categorized according to its relative "importance" with the result that the original list of skills was broken down into two lists. The first of these contained skills felt to be necessary for minimal success in reading for fourth grade students. Minimal success was not necessarily equated with grade level achievement. A child who had mastered these minimum skills and whose reading vocabulary was sufficiently advanced, would be able to handle so-called fourth grade level material. It would be possible, however, for a child to master these skills without having the necessary depth in vocabulary to enable him to comfortably work at grade level. The second list of skills went beyond those considered requisite for minimum competence. These two lists formed the basis for this part of Mr. Tuttle's program. Instruction related to those skills felt to be essential was teacher-led while an independent study approach was used for the more advanced skills. In both cases, a diagnostic-prescriptive plan was employed.

Several additional preparational steps were necessary before the program could get under way. Diagnostic devices, prescriptive materials and mastery tests were needed for each skill. Another important preparatory step was the designing and production of record forms for students and teacher to use in keeping track of progress. The independent study program was developed first since it was necessary to have the entire program prepared before it could be introduced to students. Work on these projects was done prior to the opening of school in September.

A Program for Independent Study

The bulk of this program related to comprehension skills and to the more advanced aspects of structural analysis. Twelve broad skill areas were selected for inclusion in this program.

- Advanced work with syllables and accent
- Advanced work in phonetic analysis
- Advanced work with prefixes and suffixes
- Main idea in sentence, paragraph, article
- Finding answers to questions
- Noting details and examples
- Outlining
- Figurative language and style
- Drawing conclusions and making judgments
- Organizational skills
- Dictionary skills
- Reference skills and use of library

For each skill area a learning package was prepared, with enough nonconsumable material for from four to six students to work simultaneously. Student work was guided by job sheets, and most of the activities were either self-directing and self-correcting or of an open-ended, "discovery" nature. Periodic check-points for teacher evaluation of student progress were built-in to the program and were indicated as such on the job sheets. The length of time a student would spend on a given skill varied from several days to several weeks depending on the students' work rate, the amount of time per day he devoted to the Skill Package and the amount of work contained in the package. Figure 6-8 shows a portion of the job sheet which accompanied the Outlining Package and illustrates the basic format for most of the Skill Learning Packages. The tasks listed on the Outlining Job Sheet continue in the same manner as the sample shown covering the following subsections.

1. Classifications
2. Main Topics
3. Subtopics
4. Details
5. Complete Outlines

JOB SHEET: OUTLINING

Check When Completed	Task No.	Materials Needed	Instruction
	1	Lesson Card 1: Classification	Read carefully.
	2	Practice Exercise 1	Follow directions on exercise sheet. Use answer key to check your work. Correct any errors.
	3	Practice Exercise 2	Do in same manner as Task 2.
	4	Practice Exercise 3	Do in same manner as Task 2.
	5	Practice Exercise 4	Do in same manner as Task 2.

Figure 6-8

JOB SHEET: OUTLING (Continued)

Check When Completed	Task No.	Materials Needed	Instruction
	6	Practice Exercise 5	Do in same manner as Task 2.
	7	Check-Up Exercise 1	Follow directions on exercise sheet. Give to teacher for checking.
	8	As Assigned	Do additional practice exercises if assigned by teacher.
	9	Lesson Card 2: Main Topics	Read carefully.
	10	Practice Exercise 6	Do in same manner as Task 2.
--	-----		--------------
--	-----		--------------
	14	Practice Exercise 10	Do in same manner as Task 2.
	15	Check-Up Exercise 2	Follow directions on exercise sheet. Give to teacher for checking.
	16	As Assigned	Do additional practice exercises if assigned by teacher.
--	-----		--------------
--	-----		--------------
	40	Final Test on Outlining	Ask teacher for materials and instructions.

Figure 6-8 (Continued)

These independent learning packages were used by students not engaged in teacher-led skill activities. Children were allowed to select the skills on which they wished to concentrate. No special sequence was required and each skill learning package was a complete unit. To help a child decide which package to work with, Mr. Tuttle prepared two related forms to accompany each package.

The first of these was a descriptive overview of the skill under consideration. This overview included a statement of objectives in the form of a list of specific things a child should be able to do if he had mastered the skill. A description of the kinds of tasks included in the package and a brief comment about the general value of the skill were also part of the overview.

The second form was a self-administered diagnostic test which enabled the student to evaluate his own degree of mastery of the skill. Whenever appropriate, the diagnostic form gave scores on subtests related to subsections of the learning package. Often a child would find that he was already adequately able to handle parts of the skill package but needed to do the tasks in the learning package for other parts of the skill. In such a case he could elect to do only those parts of the package pertaining to his areas of weakness. Such a procedure was felt to strengthen the child's self-evaluation ability and to strengthen the probability of meaningful self-selection of learning tasks.

Skill of the Week

The list of reading skills which Mr. Tuttle considered essential to minimum success in fourth grade became the core of a Skill of the Week Plan for instruction. Thirty-six mini-courses in specific skills were planned. Each unit, or mini-course, was designed to be completed in four sessions, allowing one day each week for mastery and diagnostic testing. Better than one-third·of these Skill of the Week Units related to phonetic analysis with heavy emphasis on work with vowel sounds. Almost one-third were devoted to work with structural analysis aspects of word attack. The remaining 12 mini-courses dealt with comprehension skills. A breakdown of the 36 Skills of the Week is given below.

I.   Phonetic Analysis

    1. Short vowel sounds—5 units
    2. Long vowel sounds—5 units
    3. Other common vowel sounds—2 units
    4. Blending word parts—2 units
    5. Rhyming words—1 unit

II. Structural Analysis

    1. Endings (s, ed, ing)—1 unit
    2. Compound words—1 unit
    3. Prefixes—2 units
    4. Suffixes—3 units
    5. Syllabication—2 units

III. Comprehension

    1. Classification—2 units
    2. Sequence—2 units
    3. Contextual clues to word meaning—2 units
    4. Main idea—2 units
    5. Finding answers to questions—1 unit
    6. Details—1 unit
    7. Drawing conclusions—2 units

A typical mini-course would start with a diagnostic test, usually teacher-made. The test was generally given on a Friday. On the following Monday, those students who had shown adequate mastery of the skill in question would begin or resume work with one of the independent learning packages discussed previously. Those students who had not mastered the skill would attend the Skill of the Week Sessions each day through Thursday. A session generally began with a teacher-led "lesson" on a particular aspect of the skill and a closely guided practice activity. As a rule, additional independent, self-correcting, follow-up practice was assigned. Care was taken to differentiate such assignments according to abilities. A given skill—for example, using the prefixes *un* and *re*—can be applied to words drawn from a second grade vocabulary list as well as to words drawn from a fourth grade list. On Friday a second test was administered to students in the Skill of the Week Group. This was a "mastery test" to check the students' progress. As part of the Friday testing, the diagnostic instrument for next week's skill would also be administered to all children in the class. In this way, the composition of the skills instruction groups changed from week to week according to test results.

A discussion of the specific components of one mini-course will serve as an illustration of the contents and procedure of the Skill of the Week Approach. We will use the first unit on classification as our example.

Lesson I and Follow-Up Practice:

1. Discussion and demonstration of some of the ways in which we could classify or group the children in the Skill of the Week Group

    boy/girl
    age
    height (above or below a given point)
    color (of hair, eyes, clothing)
    first letter of last name (A-G, H-P, Q-Z)

2. Directed practice in placing each word from a given list in one of two or three prelabeled categories. ("Here are the names of some things. Tell me if I should put this one in the Pets group, in the Flowers group or in the Food group.")

3. Independent, self-correcting exercises of the same nature as those used in directed practice.

Lesson II and Follow-Up Practice

1. Discussion and demonstration of some ways in which a list of words could be classified:

    kind of thing named by word
    first letter of word
    vowel sounds
    number of syllables
    words I know/words I don't know

2. Directed practice in categorizing words according to vowel sounds, number of syllables (also serves as review of those skills).

3. Independent, self-correcting exercises similar to those in directed practice.

Lesson III and Follow-Up Practice

1. Discussion of sentences written on chalkboard. ("Would this sentence belong in a paragraph about dogs or one about horses?", etc.)

2. Directed practice in sorting cards with printed sentences under two paragraph headings.

3. Independent, self-correcting exercises similar to directed practice using several packets of cards, each one different, which children exchange.

Lesson IV and Follow-Up Practice

1. Discussion of irrelevant sentences. ("Do all of the sentences in this paragraph belong there? Which one(s) do not belong?")

2. Directed practice in finding the sentence which does not belong in a paragraph.

3. Independent, self-correcting exercises involving a) deciding whether or not a paragraph has an irrelevant sentence and b) crossing out the extra sentence if there is one.

The mastery or check-up test on Friday included short items similar to those practiced each day plus two items using the classification skill in other, unpracticed ways. These two items are given below. (How many ways could *you* answer the first one? Can you think of several acceptable answers to the second?)

1. Read this list of words. Think of at least two different ways to classify these animals. Write your topics and copy the words under the right ones. Do this for at least two different sets of topics (or classifications).

ant	cat	eagle	man
dog	horse	bee	minnow
shark	frog	lion	canary

2. Here are some phrases. Some of them belong in the same story. Some do not belong in the story. Cross out the ones that do not belong in the story. Then write a good title for a story which would use the phrases you have left.

a very dark night	gloomy old house
howling dogs	my favorite song
two funny clowns	a sudden scream
creaking stairs	clock striking midnight
corn for dinner	going to school

In utilizing what he felt to be the best of two models, Mr. Tuttle developed a two-strand program in which work on reading skills was treated as a separate entity. Skill lessons and practice activities were not based on stories and articles contained within a given book. This enabled the children to have free range in selecting materials to read, and, at the same time, left Mr. Tuttle in charge of the developmental skills aspect of the program. Reading "for pleasure" became just that, with no strings attached. Work in skills was treated as a tool which would enable a child to handle with comfort an ever widening range of books and other reading materials, thus increasing his own possibilities for enjoyment in reading.

Summary

Neither Mrs. Richardson nor Mr. Tuttle believed that they had found all the answers to the problem of providing for the unique reading needs of all students. They did feel, however, that they had made progress in that direction. Both programs certainly had a higher degree of individualization than that found in most whole-class or traditional three-group plans.

Mrs. Richardson's program, based on a three-group orientation, utilized pupil-teams, varied amounts and kinds of teacher-directed lessons and independent activities as vehicles for differentiating the program. Mr. Tuttle started with a highly individualized approach, employing some aspects of the self-selection/conference model for that part of his program aimed at developing pupil enthusiasm for reading. His use of flexible grouping for helping children to progress in word attack and comprehension skills brought into play certain characteristics of the diagnostic-prescriptive model.

Although the differences between Mrs. Richardson's program and Mr. Tuttle's program are quite obvious, it is more important to notice the similarities. Both teachers wanted to find ways to improve their methods of handling individual differences in reading. Both programs were characterized by several valuable qualities.

- Interaction among children and between children and teacher
- Teacher awareness of each child's progress
- Work on specific skills based on need, making this kind of work more relevant
- Built-in evaluation devices
- Pupil's self-selection of some activities
- Some unstructured time
- High degree of student awareness of his own strengths, weaknesses and progress
- Flexibility in scheduling and in grouping
- A comfortable, supportive, productive atmosphere

In their search for a solution to a common problem, these two teachers illustrate that there can be more than one workable way to approach the task of providing for differentiated programs in reading.

Vitalizing Language Arts

7

Language Arts as used in education today is a blanket term covering many aspects of language production and consumption. Some schools include reading instruction in the unified language arts program, but in most cases reading is treated as a separate entity in the curriculum. Cutting across the lines of production and consumption are written and oral forms of language resulting in a matrix yielding the four major categories of the language arts program:

(1) the production of written language,
(2) the consumption of written language,
(3) the production of oral language and
(4) the consumption of oral language.

These are frequently referred to as writing, reading, speaking and listening. Each of these categories is again broken down into different types of language activities resulting in a broad and varied program generally falling under the label Language Arts.

The thought of differentiating such a multifaceted program may at first seem somewhat overwhelming. However a consideration of some of the ways to differentiate each of the programs' main components will show that it is not an impossible task. We will look first at several aspects of language production.

LANGUAGE PRODUCTION ACTIVITIES

Production of written language includes some types of activities which are often taught as separate "subjects." Spelling and hand-writing are the two major examples. Other types of activities in this category are frequently treated as "units" of study or a series of units; for example: Usage or grammar and the mechanics of writing, such as punctuation, capitalization and structure. Activities falling under the name of "creative writing" may be inserted at convenient places or periodic intervals throughout the program.

The production of oral language is likely to receive a minimum of attention in the language arts program although it is the major means of communication throughout life. Oral reporting and dramatizations represent most of the formal language activities in this category of instruction. Such activities are generally treated infrequently and in isolation.

Although general practice sees most of these aspects of language taught separately, there are many valid reasons for correlating activities. You will probably find that you already do this to some extent. A bit of divergent thinking on your part will undoubtedly reveal more opportunities for meaningful correlation.

Correlation of the language arts often makes a more flexible framework for differentiation and individualization. Specific activities for differentiating various facets of language production can be channeled to individual children or small groups as needed while maintaining an overall unity of purpose and direction.

Let us consider some of these specific language production activities.

Differentiating Instruction in Spelling

Two aspects of spelling which can easily be modified for differentiation or individualization within a classroom are the choice of words to be learned and the selection of a method or methods to be applied in the learning process. A third way in which you can differentiate spelling instruction is by modifying the rate at which you feed new words to specific children.

Choosing a list of words for a particular child involves consideration of level, or degree of difficulty, and utility. A basic rule-of-thumb is to have the words fall within the child's listening and reading vocabulary since it would be somewhat unrealistic to expect the child to learn to spell words he can neither understand nor read (decode). Lists of words at different levels of difficulty are fairly easy to come by. There are many grade-by-grade programs published commercially. State or school district syllabi print grade level lists. If you are interested in compiling your own lists, you might consider a basal reading series as one possible source for words. Most commercial programs and syllabus lists have been screened for utility. That is, words included in these lists are considered to be words which a child is likely to use in written work. You can use your own judgment in weeding out infrequently used words from the lists you build yourself.

Methods employed in learning new spelling words—or perhaps we should say in practicing new spelling words—range over a wide variety of techniques. Words may be practiced in isolation. Tracing and copying are two such techniques. A visual memory ritual may also be followed, such as: Look at the word, cover it, spell it in your mind, check, cover the word again, write the word, check it, repeat until you have written it correctly three (or five) times in a row. A rote type of oral spelling also attacks words in isolation. Many of the practice exercises in commercial programs—*i.e.*, "which words have the *long i* sound" or "write the words in alphabetical order"—use words in isolation as the basis of learning. For some children it is more effective to use a words-in-context method of practice. Using spelling words in written phrases, sentences, poems or stories helps a child make the transition from a list of words to words used comfortably in written expression. After all, isn't that the purpose for learning to spell?

Only you and the child can determine which technique or combination of techniques will work best for him. The child's attitude toward the various ways to practice coupled with your own observation and experimentation will establish guidelines for making these decisions. Occasionally, introducing a new type of practice for a short time will help retain the child's enthusiasm if this should begin to lag.

Considerations of rate will also require experimentation. A simple way to approach this is to start with a few words, perhaps six, for a week's list. Gradually add two extra words each week until the child's consistent failure to master all words indicates that he has passed his optimum load. Assuming that a child's list contains words of the right degree of difficulty, his mastery should be nearly perfect. Another way to assess the rate at which a child can learn new words is to assign a longer list of words, perhaps ten to 20, and check for how long it takes him to learn the list. Whichever approach you use, the important goal is to identify a comfortable rate of learning for each child. If you cannot start by assessing each child to this extent, try working with small groups of children and look for the rate that is comfortable for almost all of the children in a given group. For this method, you may need to accept 80-85% as a satisfactory mastery level for some of the youngsters in the group.

Using a Multi-Level Approach

Let us assume that you have decided to use a multi-level approach to differentiating instruction in spelling. Essentially this means you will utilize a commercial program, syllabi lists or other sources of materials which have been broken down into levels of difficulty, probably grade-by-grade levels. You will assign children to specific levels according to their ability to work successfully with words at those levels.

Initially your greatest concern will be to find an appropriate level for each child. Group diagnostic testing can help you in making these decisions. A fairly simple but effective method is to test everyone with about 20-25% of all the words contained in a given level and selected randomly from each lesson or unit in the program. Start with the easiest level and eliminate children from the diagnostic testing program as you find their appropriate levels for instruction. A good plan is to set a cut-off point for acceptable scores. Ninety percent or better is reasonable to expect as an indication of mastery. The first score below 90% indicates that this is probably an appropriate instructional level for the child.

Once instructional levels have been established for each child, attention can be turned to study methods, rate of progress and testing procedures. If you are using a commercially published spelling series, the method you employ may be simply to follow the lessons in the text or workbook. You may wish to substitute or supplement with other practice methods, such as those mentioned earlier, especially for students who need extra practice in order to maintain 90% mastery. Not all children working at a given level will learn new words at the same rate. You must expect some variation in the number of words learned per week or in the length of time required to learn a given number of words. However, if you notice that a child seems unusually slow at learning new words or if a child consistently falls below 90% mastery and retention of new words, you may find that he is working at the wrong level.

Testing in a multilevel program need not be a confusing and cumbersome task. Children, working in pairs, can give each other pretests and posttests for regular lessons. Periodic tests for evaluating retention can be given to individual students by children from a higher level or by using prerecorded cassette tapes. Occasionally, major check-up tests can be administered by the teacher to all children in a given level of the program. Words included on this test should be drawn only from lessons which have been completed by all children in the group.

Personalized Spelling Lists

A further step in individualizing spelling instruction is the provision of personalized lists of words for some or all of the children in your class. Words for a specific child may be selected in a number of ways. Modification and extension of the diagnostic testing program described above is a good way to begin such a list. When the child scores less than 90% on the diagnostic test, he can be assigned to that level, at least temporarily. His personalized list of words may be compiled of all those words he has missed in diagnostic testing up to this point. Further testing of the remaining 75-80% of words at his level will reveal other words to add to his list. Words selected from reading vocabulary lists, other subject areas and the child's own interests may also become part of his personalized list. Subsequent testing at the next level in spelling provides an additional source for new words as they are needed. Let the student become involved in the selection of words for his own list as much as possible.

The personalized list approach to spelling instruction allows for flexibility in selecting effective word practicing techniques and in establishing a comfortable rate. Pupil-team testing can be employed as easily as in the multi-level approach. With the use of personalized lists, children concentrate on new words and do not spend time doing practice exercises with words they already can spell. A high degree of motivation results from pupil involvement in the planning and compiling aspects of this program. Such advantageous characteristics as these make the personalized list approach well worth considering.

Individualizing the Handwriting Program

Many handwriting programs stress conformity of style as well as legibility. This is perhaps unfortunate. The time we spend trying to force children to use a particular style of curlicues, or lack of curlicues, might be better spent in improving legibility and fluency. What difference does it really make in the long run whether the upper case cursive letter **T** is written like this *J* or this *𝒥* or this *𝒯* ? Slavish insistence on conformity to a particular style or system of handwriting dampens motivation and inhibits the development and improvement of personalized styles.

Acceptance of personalized styles does not mean lowering the standards of legibility. We can permit a child to use a vertical rather than a forward slant if that is the orientation which seems to come naturally for him, and still ask for uniformity of slant. Uniformity of slant becomes a matter of a given child's consistency in using his preferred method rather than an insistence that all children conform to the same slant. In a similar manner we can insist that written letters are clearly distinguishable, leaving no doubt as to whether a given letter is meant to be an "a" an "o" or a "u" without demanding that one child's "a" be congruent with all other "a"s. By permitting personalized variations in styles, we can give the child more of the scheduled handwriting time to devote to the development of habits of legibility, internal consistency and ultimately to increased fluency.

Individualization in handwriting instruction can also take the form of differentiated practice activities. Practice techniques and material used for practicing each technique offer opportunities for differentiating the practice activities.

Some children may benefit from tracing, others may do well by copying a model. Whenever possible, use a child's own "best" work to serve as his model for tracing or copying. If you must make the model for him, try to have it conform with his own developing style, especially with regard to slant. Handwriting practice books and programmed workbooks offer possible sources of model-aided practice for some children. Since these materials stress conformity to a specific style, they would not be suitable for those children whose personalized styles differ markedly from that of the printed program. Models for tracing and copying are devices used in the beginning stages of practice and should be eliminated as soon as possible. Here again, you will find that individual differences occur in the amount of model-aided practice a child needs before his mental image of the letters enables him to branch out on his own.

Personalized Handwriting Practice

Additional opportunities for differentiating handwriting instruction can be found in the specific content of practice material and in rate or timing factors. Children's needs will vary with regard to specific letters requiring concentrated or extended practice and the amount of time necessary for the practice. To insist that all children spend a given amount of time or a given number of lessons working on a specific letter or letters is not consistent with the concept of individualization and results in much wasted time for many youngsters.

A kit of practice exercises can be prepared in such a way as to permit the flexibility and self-selection necessary for personalized practice. Exercises in the kit can be organized according to the content of the exercises as well as the type of practice needed. Content could be categorized according to the following classifications:

1. Individual Letters
2. Families of Letters (a, c, d, g, q)
3. Generalized Practice (all letters)
4. Extension Practice (student-composed work)

Within the first two categories, sections can be designated—perhaps by letter, number or color coding—according to type of practice, such as tracing, model-aided copying and copying from a typed exercise.

Your kit could be made with 5 x 8 index cards which would make storage and accessibility to students a simple matter. Practice exercises for the *Families of Letters* category might include the following set of practice cards.

Tracing —one green card with letters in isolation (no. 1)
        —one green card with short words featuring letters (no. 2)

Model-aided—one pink card with letters in isolation (no. 1)
        —three pink cards with short words (nos. 2-4)
        —three pink cards with phrases or sentences (nos. 5-7)

Typed exercises—five yellow cards with words (nos. 1-5)
        —five yellow cards with phrases and sentences (nos. 6-10)
        —five yellow cards with short stories or paragraphs featuring the letters (nos. 11-15)

Similar exercises could be included for the category of *Individual Letters*, with each letter of the alphabet having its own set of exercises, including some with capital letters. Fewer practice cards per letter than the number suggested for *Families of Letters* may be found to be adequate.

Generalized Practice and *Extension Practice* would not need tracing or model-aided practice exercises. Here you may wish to provide ten or more practice cards under each of three headings: easy practice, regular practice and difficult practice. Length of words, complexity of sentences and length of overall exercise would be determining factors in assigning the easy, regular or difficult heading to each exercise.

Sources of content for *Generalized Practice* exercises could include several of the following types of passages:

1. Jokes
2. Riddles
3. Humerous selections from books
4. Poems

5. Descriptions (of animals, people, etc.)
6. Instructions (how to make a ____)
7. "Mood" passages (spooky, exciting, peaceful, etc.)
8. Short, short stories
9. Social studies selections
10. Science experiments or explanations
11. Math problems
12. Brain teasers

Practice exercises for *Extension Practice* would be more in the nature of suggestions for sentences, poems, paragraphs and stories which the students would compose themselves. This aspect of practice is more closely related to the habit of using good handwriting in everyday school work.

Self-Evaluation and Student-Directed Practice

Involve the pupil in evaluation of his own handwriting. When he has produced a specimen of his "very best" handwriting, have him first identify those specific letters or problem areas which he feels need improvement. If he misses one which you feel needs extra practice have him include it with those he has pinpointed and tell him why you feel it should be included. Have children maintain a periodic check of their handwriting progress and keep a record of practice needed. It can be as simple as a monthly checklist of letters needing practice, such as the chart given below.

Date of Evaluation	a	b	c	d	e	f	g	h	i	j	k	l	m	n	o	---	z
1.																	
2.																	
3.																	
4.																	
5.																	
6.																	
7.																	
8.																	
9.																	
10.																	

This student-kept record presents an immediate visual picture of progress as well as an indication of letters currently needing practice. Using the information a student has shown on this chart, he can plan a program of corrective practice of his own personal handwriting demons using the kit described in the previous section of this chapter. A Student Practice Record Sheet can be used to guide him in his program of self-directed practice. A form similar to the one which follows may be used for this purpose.

STUDENT PRACTICE RECORD SHEET FOR_____

DATE_____

Letters	Tracing (Green)		Model (Pink)			Typed Exercises (Yellow)				
	1	2	1	2	3	1	2	3	4	5
	1	2	1	2	3	1	2	3	4	5
	1	2	1	2	3	1	2	3	4	5
	1	2	1	2	3	1	2	3	4	5
	1	2	1	2	3	1	2	3	4	5
	1	2	1	2	3	1	2	3	4	5
	1	2	1	2	3	1	2	3	4	5
	1	2	1	2	3	1	2	3	4	5
	1	2	1	2	3	1	2	3	4	5

Families	Tracing (Green)		Model (Pink)			Typed Exercises (Yellow)				
	1	2	1			1	2	3	4	5
			2	3	4	6	7	8	9	10
			5	6	7	11	12	13	14	15
	1	2	1			1	2	3	4	5
			2	3	4	6	7	8	9	10
			5	6	7	11	12	13	14	15

On this type of record the student would enter the letters he needs to practice. When more than one letter from a "family" needs practice, he would also enter the family under the second part of the form. Numbers listed under Tracing, Model and Typed Exercises indicate the numbers on exercise cards found in the personalized practice kit. The student circles the numbers of the exercises he plans to do. When he has completed an exercise, he marks an X through the circle. In the section of the form relating to families of letters, each row of numbers refers to a different content of practice. For example, under Typed Exercises, 1-5 are word cards, 6-10 are phrase and sentence cards and 11-15 are story or paragraph cards. Thus a student could elect to do cards 1, 2, 3, 6, 7 and 14, thereby providing himself with a variety of practice exercises.

As a student's "very best" specimens improve, shift the emphasis to everyday usage of good handwriting. Again involve the child in self-evaluation. Have him compare his best handwriting specimens with samples of his everyday work. He should attempt to discover where carelessness, hurry or indifference cause him to lower his own standards of excellence and seek ways to overcome these poor habits. A sense of pride in his own work and active involvement in the evaluation of it will increase motivation for this kind of individualized practice. The *Generalized* and *Extension* categories of the personalized practice kit can be used for this aspect of handwriting practice. Practice Record Sheets can be designed along the lines of the one illustrated above.

One word of caution regarding the integration of cursive handwriting practice with other aspects of the curriculum is important at this point. Do not insist that a child employ cursive handwriting in the performance of other language arts, social studies or science activities until he has mastered the handwriting skills. To do so is to impose a double task on him and is likely to result in his attending primarily to either the handwriting aspect of the assignment *or* the subject content of the assignment simply because he does not yet have the ability to deal with both simultaneously. If the child *wants* to use cursive writing in his other school work, you will probably wish to take advantage of his enthusiasm, but to insist upon it before he is ready will bring frustration and lower motivation.

Varying the Emphasis on Language Mechanics

A fourth grade teacher will find among her students a wide range of abilities in the use of the mechanics of written language. The same will be true, in varying degrees, for teachers at higher or lower grade levels. A few children may be able to express themselves in well-organized, grammatically correct, easily understood and correctly capitalized and punctuated paragraphs or compositions, while others cannot correctly write a complete sentence. How can a teacher design a language arts program which will avoid unnecessary exposure for those students already sophisticated in the mechanics of written language, and, at the same time, provide a structure for systematically building a stronger framework of acceptable written language for other students?

One third grade teacher utilized a multigroup plan in connection with a grade level English text. Another teacher approached this problem by designing and producing a variety of packages of short-term learning activities for specific aspects of language mechanics for her intermediate grade students. A closer look at each of these methods will reveal many ideas and techniques which can be adapted to other grade levels and other classroom situations.

A Multigroup Plan

The multigroup plan discussed here represents a teacher's first attempt to differentiate language instruction. Since this was but her third year of teaching, her first year at the third grade level and her first year in a new school district, Miss Foster planned to move slowly into differentiating instruction and to rely heavily on the 32 copies of a third grade English series, which she found on her classroom bookshelves, for the content of her program. She decided to use a three-group plan, similar to that used for reading instruction, for one part of the program, and a conventional whole class approach for another part. After studying the overall contents of the English text, Miss Foster identified those sections which dealt with written language for use with the three groups. Oral language and other aspects of the program were to be handled in whole class situations.

A bit of preliminary exploratory work with the children suggested a possible grouping plan. A small group of six youngsters appeared likely to move smoothly and rapidly through the written language parts of the program. A larger group containing 15 children was felt to be ready to start work in the written language activities but was expected to need more practice and reinforcement than the first group, and was thus expected to move more slowly in the program. The remaining ten children were believed to require additional oral language experiences before they would be ready to move into written language activities.

During the first three days of each week, English time was devoted to the multigroup activities. The last two days were used for whole class participation in the oral language experiences. Miss

Foster met with only two groups on any one day. Generally she met with the readiness group on each of the three days, with the large group on two days and with the accelerated group once each week. For all but the readiness group, she was able to use material in the grade level text for lessons and follow-up practice. This material was supplemented by additional activities drawn from teachers' editions of two or three other third-grade English texts. Providing suitable activities for the readiness group required greater ingenuity. Teachers' editions from lower level English series and from various reading series offered many suggestions for building oral language skills and for some introductory writing activities. About halfway through the year, carefully selected and reinforced written language activities from the regular third grade text were added to the program for the readiness group.

Although Miss Foster's attempts to modify the language program were quite modest, she was able to alter the program by differentiating rate of progress, frequency of activities and content of materials and activities, thus varying the emphasis on written language aspects of the program.

Packaged Learning Activities

A fifth grade teacher faced with a wide range of abilities and skills in language mechanics spent considerable time in packaging independent learning activities at different levels of difficulty. Each set of activities dealt with a specific aspect of language mechanics. Level I materials included four sets of activities.

- Writing Sentences
- Capital Letters
- Using Periods
- Word Usage I

Level II included sets of activities such as the following:

- Basic Commas
- Better Sentences
- Paragraphs
- Word Usage II
- Outlining
- Informal Letters

Materials in Level III contained such sets of activities as:

- Writing Conversation
- Advanced Punctuation

- Word Usage III
- Compositions and Articles
- Business Letters
- Advanced Sentence Structure

as well as sets on the various parts of speech.

The activities contained in each set of packaged materials were designed or chosen to be self-directing, and, whenever possible, self-correcting, making them suitable for independent or pupil-team learning. Teacher observations and pretesting were used to determine a student's need for specific sets of activities. A child was not necessarily confined to a given level of materials. Thus a student might start with Basic Commas, a Level II set, following this with work on Word Usage I.

All sets of materials at a given level contained activities utilizing a few basic formats. At Level I all packaged sets included Concept Cards, Practice Cards, Extension Cards, Review Cards and Evaluation Cards. The Writing Sentences Package is a good example of the activity sets at this level. The materials included in this package are listed below.

Re: Complete sentences
   10 Concept Cards
   10 Practice Cards
   10 Extension Cards

Re: Starting sentences with capitals
   5 Concept Cards
   5 Practice Cards
   5 Extension Cards

Re: Ending "telling" sentences with periods
   5 Concept Cards
   5 Practice Cards
   5 Extension Cards

Re: Ending "asking" sentences with question marks
   5 Concept Cards
   5 Practice Cards
   5 Extension Cards

Re: Making sentences more interesting
   10 Concept Cards
   10 Practice Cards
   10 Extension Cards

Re: General review and evaluation
>5 Review Cards
>10 Practice Cards
>3 Evaluation Cards

An example of a Concept Card for Complete Sentences is given in Figure 7-1.

Writing Sentences   *Concept Card*
                                                   Complete Sentences–3

Each of these is a complete sentence.
1. Tom and Mary went to the circus.
2. A small gray kitten played with yarn.
3. Mother ran home.
4. I walked.
5. He can go with me.

None of these is a complete sentence.
1. A little brown and white spotted dog.
2. Went home from school last night.
3. Two of the boys and three of the girls.
4. After the party was over.
5. Me to go to the store for you.

Which of these are complete sentences?
1. Some of the boys in my class.
2. Jane ran.
3. I will help you with your work.
4. Played in the sandbox all day.
5. She is my very best friend.

Answers are given on the back of this card.

Figure 7-1

All sets of activities for Level II contained the five card formats used at Level I plus Reference Cards which listed book titles and page numbers where explanatory material and extra practice could be found. A typical Practice Card for Level II sets taken from the Basic Commas Package is shown in Figure 7-2.

Packages in Level III utilized the six formats used at Level II plus Model Cards and Proofreading Cards. Model Cards, as the name implies, contained samples of correctly written items which were too long to include on Concept Cards. Proofreading Cards had examples of written work containing some errors. The student's task was to

Basic Commas

Use these words	in these sentences. Watch the commas!
1. red yellow and blue	1. Mary's favorite colors are . . . .
2. Don Bill Sue and I	2. . . . . went home early.
3. one two or three	3. You may have . . . . cookies.
4. one lion one elephant two monkeys and five seals	4. We saw . . . . at the zoo.
5. A red bike a blue wagon two baseballs a tent and five fishing rods	5. Jimmy counted . . . . at the toy store.

Use the Answer Key for this Practice Card to check your work.

Figure 7-2

Writing Conversation

Correct all errors you find in this passage.

"Hi, Mary." called Beth. "What are you doing?

"I'm making a list of things I am going to buy at the store" Mary responded.

"When are you goint to go shopping"? asked Beth?

Probably tomorrow morning. Do you want to go with me?

"I would like to go. I'll ask my mother if she has any shopping for me to do" responded Beth eagerly.

"Okay, then" said Mary "I'll see you tomorrow morning at ten!

Use the Answer Key for this Proofreading Card to check your work.

Figure 7-3

identify and correct all errors found on the card. An example of a Proofreading Card for Writing Conversation is found in Figure 7-3.

Some of the activities included in these packages, especially those on Extension Cards and Evaluation Cards, did not lend themselves to the use of answer keys for self-correction. In such cases, the student found a partner or asked a designated "student checker" to check his work. Certain activities required that the completed work be given to the teacher for checking. This enabled the teacher to keep posted on pupil progress and to okay movement to another set of activities.

To introduce new activities or concepts, the teacher frequently met with small groups of students. On occasion whole class sessions would include related teacher-led lessons, generally with regard to ways of working with the packages and specific formats within them. Most of the time students worked individually or with a partner, progressing at a comfortable rate and level.

The exercises and activities contained in this program were not new or unique. However, the way in which they were organized, packaged and utilized made them a valuable contribution to this teacher's language arts program.

Providing Alternatives in Creative Writing

Creative writing by its very nature is a highly individual experience. Individualizing this aspect of language instruction will virtually take care of itself if the classroom teacher will maintain an open mind and will expect, encourage and accept widely divergent finished products from her students' creative writing endeavors. To hold differing expectations regarding the frequency, quantity, quality, content, style and form of the written product sounds easier than it really is. One must be quite well acquainted with all aspects of a child's life in order to make a reasonable judgment about the creative writing which he might be expected to produce. The encouragement of diversity in children's creative writing provides the teacher with an opportunity for some creativity and divergent thinking of her own. Gone are the days of mass assignments such as "Today we will write a story about a Halloween Adventure" or "This would be a good day to write poems about Spring." Accepting each child's written offering is directly related to holding differing expectations and will often require a great deal of perceptive judgment and tact on the part of the teacher.

Invitations to "Creative" Writing

If we think of creative writing as writing which expresses the writer's own thinking or feelings, we will realize how important it is to avoid imposing limitations or requirements such as length, topic or literary form. On the other hand, it is highly desirable to offer a wide variety of motivational *invitations* to writing providing such invitations carry with them complete freedom for self-selection and the option of refusing the invitation entirely. Invitations to creative writing can take the form of a tangible object or an idea.

One teacher assembled several dozen one-of-a-kind invitations to creative writing which she presented to her class in sets of from eight to 15 at a time at irregular intervals. To prepare these invitations, the teacher first collected many illustrations which she felt would be intriguing and highly motivational for her students. She was able in a short time to assemble a very sizeable collection from back issues of children's magazines, discarded reading and library books, comic strips, adult magazines, coloring books and even gift wrapping paper. Each illustration was cut out in an interesting shape using irregular forms whenever possible. Each was then framed by colored construction paper of a similar form and mounted, together with lined composition paper in an interesting shape on a larger sheet of shaped construction paper.

From time to time several of these illustrated "invitations" were arranged on a low bulletin board. Children in the class were invited to study the illustrations at their leisure and to write a story, poem, paragraph or a collection of interesting words, phrases or sentences about one of the pictures if they wished. When only one child elected to write about a given illustration, his work could be copied directly onto the lined paper mounted on the construction paper. If more than one child wrote about an illustration, they could copy their work on unmounted composition paper which would be displayed one at a time on the bulletin board invitation. An example of these invitations to creative writing is illustrated in Figure 7-4.

Invitations to expanded thinking can be fun for teachers and children alike. School-age children, especially those beyond the primary grades, are so often inhibited in their creative expression by a desire to satisfy what they feel to be adult standards of representativeness. They want their drawings of trees to "look like" trees and they want their poems to "sound like" poems, which being interpreted means rhyme takes precedent over rhythm and meaning. We can provide opportunities for children to go beyond representational stereotypes and to use abstractions, symbolism and expressionism in creative writing if we avoid getting all wrappped up in terminology and complicated concepts. We can use *ideas* as invitations to expanded thinking and to explorations in writing.

Invitation to Creative Writing

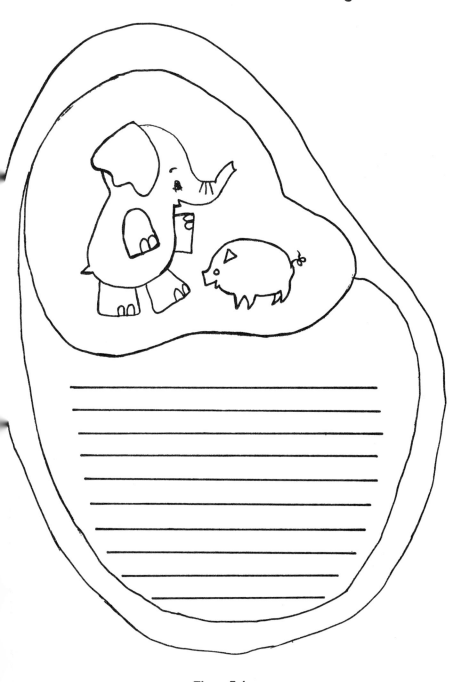

Figure 7-4

For example, take the color *red*. Red is not in itself a tangible object and yet it is something familiar to even a very young school child. Using red, or any color, as a point of departure, we can encourage children to expand upon such ideas as these:

If purple were an object I could see, what would purple be?

If green were something I could touch, how would green feel to my hand?

If orange were a place, where would orange be?

If blue were edible, how would blue taste?

If yellow were a feeling (emotion), how would yellow feel?

If red were a sound, what would I hear when I listened to red?

The Art of Accepting

A real need exists for accepting the child's creative writing offering with an honest enthusiasm which will convey your awareness of the quality of his offering in relation to a reasonable expectation for him and at the same time will leave open the door of his desire to continue writing and to continue improving his writing. Nothing motivates additional improvement like acknowledgment of improvement already made. And nothing motivates additional productivity like recognition of current products. The acknowledgment of improvement should be specific and is effective when done on a one-to-one, face-to-face basis. Recognition of current writing products can be more general and may take the form of visually sharing the product with others in the classroom or with the school in general.

Sometimes it is difficult to comment honestly and constructively about the quality of a student's work. Consider the case of the sixth grade teacher who had just received a "story" from a student who was definitely a reluctant writer. This was his second attempt of the year and just barely met the "one paper per quarter" quota deadline. The paper contained three sentences to the effect that he played football, it was a good game and he liked to play it. How does a teacher react in a situation like this; what does she say to the student? One suggestion is to identify the most positive strength in the paper and use this as the focus of your comments. This teacher's conversation with the student went something like this.

Teacher: You chose a good topic to write on.

Student: (no response)

Teacher: It's always a good idea to write about something you have had some experience with.

Student: (no response)
Teacher: Do you play any other sports?
Student: Yeah. I play baseball and sometimes basketball. I don't like basketball much, though.
Teacher: Oh, why not?
Student: Oh, I don't know. I like to be outdoors. It's all right if you're just shooting a few baskets outside, but I don't like it much when you have to play it in the gym.
Teacher: Perhaps sometime you'd write something about one of the other sports you play. Maybe you could even tell a little about *why* you like it or don't like it . . . sort of like what you have been telling me about basketball just now. That would make it more interesting to read.
Student: Yeah, well . . . maybe I will.

I'm sure this conversation was not the highlight of the day for either participant. However, it was infinitely better than such a comment as, "Only three sentences, John? It seems to me a sixth grader could do better than that. You had better take it back and do it over, and try to do a better job this time." The first conversation had something positive to say about the paper, gave the student an opportunity to identify possible topics for future papers, and made concrete suggestions for improvement on the next paper. The second conversation would merely put down the student and give him little incentive for future endeavors.

Public recognition of written work may be a casual affair or may be done with more ceremony. Displaying finished papers with a flourish is best done only occasionally or it may lose its impact. Regular daily or weekly sharing of written work may be less formal in nature without delegating the compositions to obscurity. Some method of regular, periodic sharing plus a few special occasions spaced throughout the year should serve to recognize student efforts satisfactorily and, at the same time, maintain or stimulate continued productivity. Here are a few suggestions which you might want to consider for adaptation to your own classroom needs.

Portfolios—Large three-ring notebooks or folded oak tag can be used to make portfolios into which children's creative writing products may be placed. These may become part of the classroom library or may occupy a special place in the room.

Portfolios can be made for specific types of creative writing, or each child could have his own portfolio. You may want children to put their own papers into the portfolios as work is completed or you may wish to see it first. If you do have the papers given to you first, it would be a nice reminder about the portfolios if periodically you comment about the titles and types of material you are currently adding to the portfolios.

Card Catalog—A classroom index system can be devised to record information about stories, poems and other papers written by your students. Cards might be arranged according to topic or type of contents—*i.e.* animal stories, science fiction, biography, poetry, humorous, etc. A more elaborate catalog could be similar to a library card catalog with cross references according to topic, title and author. The written work itself may be filed alphabetically by author, or your students might enjoy designing their own system.

Add-a-Line Poems—Use the bulletin board as a place to create *and* display poetry in the making. On each of several attractively mounted sheets of lined paper, write the title, and, if you wish, the first line or two of a poem. Let children contribute to the developing poems by adding one line or a few lines as they are "inspired." Suggest that they read the poem as far as it goes before composing and adding their own lines.

Classroom Book— This is the same idea as the add-a-line poem expanded into a developing book with an add-a-chapter feature. Specific characters should be identified and named (by the children) before any chapters are written. You might read aloud books such as A.A. Milne's *Winnie-the-Pooh* (E.P. Dutton & Co., Inc.) to serve as a model of books containing chapters which are complete short stories in themselves. The classroom book thus becomes a collection of short stories about the same group of characters. As new chapters are added to the book, their authors may be asked to tell the class the title and general idea of the new adventure or situation in their story.

Literary Gallery—Toward the end of each report card marking period, you have a perfect opportunity to combine an activity in self-evaluation on the part of students with a special occasion display of written work. As the semester or quarter progresses, have each child maintain a collection of his own creative writing. You might use portfolios or large manila envelopes for this purpose. Near the end of the report period, have each child reread his papers and arrange them according to his opinion of their merit. Each child should then select one of his best works to be displayed with a flourish in a classroom literary gallery. The selected work should be attractively framed or mounted in some manner suggesting the content of the paper. For example, a poem about flowers could be mounted on a large green circle and surrounded by a wreath of three-dimensional paper flowers, or a circus story might be mounted inside the fold-out doors of a circus tent or superimposed on a three-dimensional circus wagon. If possible, you might wish to share your literary gallery with others in the school by displaying it in a hall or cafeteria.

Children's Magazines—A really significant and dramatic way to recognize children's work is to suggest that your students might like to submit a story, poem or article to one of the commercially published magazines written by and/or for children. This is a good once-a-year project. Perhaps in the spring you might have interested students select a good paper they have created during the year which they wish to have sent to the publisher. Or some children might prefer to write something new especially for this purpose. If possible such material should be typed, double-spaced, and may be sent as a single package as long as each contribution is typed on a separate page with the author's name and address. You may find students' mothers may be willing to volunteer for the task of typing. Be sure to explain to your students that it is likely to be quite a time before they hear anything about their manuscripts.

Whatever techniques you decide to employ for the purposes of inviting and recognizing the creative writing efforts of your students, the key to individualization lies in your willingness and ability to expect, encourage and accept widely differing finished products.

LANGUAGE CONSUMPTION ACTIVITIES

Language consumption aspects of the language arts program generally include such activities as reading poetry, reference and library skills, listening to stories and something called "reading for pleasure" or "literature appreciation." Choral reading, some forms of dramatization and oral interpretation of literature (often thought of as reading the story or poem aloud) may also be considered language consumption activities, at least in part. Too often such aspects of language are slighted or even overlooked in the school program. How can we find ways, not only to increase opportunities for children to engage in these activities, but to provide alternatives which allow for individual differences in experience, interest and skills? A discussion of two rather broad areas of language consumption will suggest a few possibilities and start you off on your own creative planning for more, better and differentiated activities.

Opportunities for Enjoying Literature

The key word here is *opportunities*. By providing a variety of opportunities to explore different forms of literature and by permitting children to engage in self-selection of activities, you automatically provide considerable accommodation for individual differences. In creating opportunities for enjoying literature you must provide several things: the literature to be enjoyed, suggestions for ways to share enjoyment, times and places for the enjoyment and sharing to take place and significant options for choosing the when, which, how and how much of participation in the activities.

Oral Interpretation of Literature

There are two sides to the coin of oral interpretation of literature. On the one side is the relatively passive activity of listening to someone else's interpretation of a story or poem. A *See-and-Hear Station* can be set up in one small area of the room. Filmstrips, tapes and records and the necessary audio-visual hardware may be made available for children's use. Copies of books or poems are nice to follow visually while listening.

The second side of the coin is the more active involvement of interpreting and sharing aloud this interpretation of a story or poem. Children will enjoy scheduling a story hour session for the purpose of reading aloud to interested classmates. A weekly list of times when such sessions may be scheduled could be posted on an activities bulletin board. Children who wish to read aloud may insert their names and the titles of their selections next to the times they wish to hold a story hour. A *Story Nook* containing a specially decorated story-teller's chair would be a good place for such sessions to take place. Oral interpretation of literature may also take the form of puppet shows or playlets. Activities such as these could be scheduled on the same list with story hour sessions.

Sources of Literature

If literature is to be enjoyed by children, it must be easily available to them. A once-a-week trip to the school library is not in itself an adequate means of making literature available although it may be an important part of a larger plan. A classroom collection is necessarily more limited in scope and quantity, but it has the essential advantage of immediate availability at the moment of interest or readiness. Many publishers produce series of grade-level literature anthologies for elementary school children. Stock your classroom collection with at least two copies of each book from several series to provide variety as well as a range of reading levels. Two or more copies of each book permits paired oral reading of stories, plays and poems. A *Poetry Box* of poems printed on cards or colored construction paper and filed according to type of subject makes an inviting source of reading material. You may want to feature a *Specialty of the Month* in your literature collection with a special display of the month's featured literature: legends and myths, plays, fairy tales, poetry, biography, fantasy, short stories or a particular author.

On-Going Display Projects

During the middle elementary grades many children develop a keen interest in reading biographies. Take advantage of this interest in your literature campaign. A continually developing bulletin board or display based on *Interesting Personalities* will stimulate reading as well as serve as an avenue for sharing. Be sure to have several sources of information about each personality being currently featured. Encourage children to add their contributions to the display by providing space for illustrations, quotes, dates and events, inventions or discoveries and other interesting facts. A periodic survey with the whole class to call attention to new additions to the display will provide recognition for the contributions already made and encourage new ones.

You can devise similar plans for having older or younger pupils add to a developing literature bulletin board. The same idea of interesting personalities could be extended for younger children to include fictional characters or to embrace a whole category of types of fictional characters such as interesting animal characters or interesting elves, fairies and "little people." Older students might enjoy turning the display into a kind of visual quiz game. Viewers would be presented with facts, quotes and illustrations to be identified with a particular personality, type of literature or author. Outlets for sharing, such as these developing displays, give a little added excitement to the pleasures of reading literature and provide opportunities for children of widely differing abilities to take part in a single unifying activity.

Literature-Oriented Fun Time Activities

A variety of games, parties, projects and other fun-type activities can be designed to feature a particular story, fictional character or type of book. Here are ten suggestions to get your thinking started along these lines.

1. Build a many-sectioned shadow box (or buy an ecology box) to hang on a wall in the classroom or library. Have students fill the compartments with items they have made or collected to create a *nostalgia box* for a particular story character.

2. Children can draw shapes of story characters on oaktag and use them as patterns for cutting out cookies or decorating a sheet cake to be served as refreshments at a *book party*. Decorations for the party, invitations (to parents or children in another class) and paper-and-pencil games should be related to the featured story. Prizes for games can also be book related.

3. A *Who Am I?* game is fun to play and requires only a short period of time. Print the names of story characters on strips of paper, one name for each child in the room. Name strips are pinned to the back of each child's clothing. Each child then circulates and asks questions (to be answered only by "yes," "no" or "I don't know") of others in an effort to guess who he is. A time limit may be set after which each person writes down the name he thinks is on his back. He may then remove his name sign and check.

4. Have a special *holiday party* for some story character. Plan refreshments and activities suitable for the "guest of honor." Activities might include trimming a Christmas tree with ornaments meaningful to the character, making suitable birthday cards, creating Halloween masks or costumes of special friends of the character or of the character himself and packing an Easter basket or going-away package with goodies the story character might enjoy.

5. Set aside a corner of the classroom and create a *walk-in diorama* of some special setting from a story. Settings such as Pooh's 100 Aker Wood, Wilbur's barn, Charlie's chocolate factory or McGrew's Zoo are possibilities you might wish to consider.

6. Some children may enjoy making *models* of story characters, buildings or objects. Models of characters can take the form of sculpture, paper dolls or real dolls dressed for a specific event in the story. Animal homes, castles, boats, space ships, islands, laboratories, etc. offer good subject material for other types of models.

7. Plan an outdoor *picnic* featuring food and games appropriate to a given book. Scavenger hunts, treasure hunts and races or

contests can be adapted for many stories. Unique story-appropriate activities for *Winnie, the Pooh* [by A.A. Milne (Dutton)] could include a "haycorn hunt," a balloon race, a game of racing sticks down a brook, a "heffalump trap" building contest or a treasure hunt for Eeyore's lost tail.

8. Have children design a *board game* to be played with dice, a spinner or a set of cards. The game should feature characters and events from a given book or type of book.

9. Prepare ditto masters of student-drawn outline pictures of story characters and events. Assemble copies of these illustrations to create a *coloring book*. Illustrations may be arranged sequentially and captions may be added by each student as he works in his own copy of the coloring book.

10. Plan a literature *costume party* featuring a particular type of book—animal stories, fairy tales, legends, etc. Have children work together in groups. Each group should select a specific book or story of the type being featured. Children in that group then prepare costumes of characters from that story. Costumes are worn at the party and a short skit or charade depicting an event from the book may be presented. Children may then try to guess books and characters being illustrated.

Reference and Library Skills

Much of the language consumption activity provided in today's schools is geared toward information seeking and comprehension. Toward this end, reading programs, English texts and in-library instruction all approach the task of helping children learn how to use reference materials effectively. The best timing for this instruction is at the point of need. A child who is looking for specific information to help him with a project has a certain amount of built-in readiness for an individualized lesson on the use of an index or the card catalog. Unfortunately, the librarian and the classroom teacher cannot always be on tap for each child at the appropriate moment. To supplement this on-the-spot instruction, we try to arrange for some type of generalized practice in the use of reference and library skills. Too often, this takes the form of whole class activities using workbook pages or worksheet exercises on "How to Use the Table of Contents" or "Dictionary Skills." A more valuable activity would be one which requires the child to actually refer to books and other reference materials (rather than excerpts printed on a workbook page) in the exercise of the task. Several small groups of children can be working at various tasks encompassing several reference skills and at different levels of difficulty. Five such activities are described briefly below. These activities provide at least as much practice as conventional workbook exercises and have the added advantage of active use of reference books and the enjoyment of a game type format. It would be reasonable for all of these activities to be taking place simultaneously in a single classroom.

Hidden Message—The student uses the Table of Contents for a given book to help him locate the hidden message. A clue for each word in the message directs the student to a particular page in the book. On that page, he will find the secret word underlined, circled or identified in some other quickly obvious way. Clues may be similar to these.
1. Look at the third page of the chapter about pioneers.
2. See the last page in the first chapter in Part II.

Clues should be given in the proper sequence so that the hidden message unfolds in order, word by word.

Out of Order—A packet of 12 cards is given to a group of two, three or four children. Each card contains a printed word. The cards are shuffled and dealt out face down to the players. The first player selects any one of his cards and places it on the chalk tray, a table or on the floor. The second player selects any one of his cards and places it next to the first card, keeping the cards in alphabetical order. Players take turns until all cards have been "played" by placing them alphabetically. Each player then uses a dictionary to check the accuracy of the total arrangement. The game may be quite simple with words such as red, orange, yellow, green, etc. Or select several words which start with the same set of letters (catastrophe, catapult, catacomb, catabolism, cataract, etc.) if you want the game to be more difficult. More than 12 cards may be used, but it makes the checking task more tedious. Two games with two different sets of 12 cards is more fun and just as much practice as one game with 24 cards.

Scavenger Hunt—Prepare a list of about 20 terms which will serve as the objects to be "found" by students playing this game. Students use the index in a given book to find their objects and write the page number (or numbers) next to that item on the list. Several children of similar ability may want to compete with each other in doing this task. A good incentive is to work for accuracy rather than speed. Terms included on the list might be similar to these.

1. Relief map of Uruguay
2. Description of strip mining
3. Table of information about irrigation farming
4. Definition of raw material

Detectives—To play this game, children will need to go to the library where they can use the card catalog. You will probably want to send them one at a time to avoid bottlenecks. The student is told that a mystery surrounds the identity of a missing person. He is handed a card containing the first in a series of clues which will eventually lead to the solution of the mystery. He should carry this card containing the first clue with him throughout his search. All other clue cards must be left where he finds them. He may jot down any notes on the card he carries. If he loses his way, he must go back to a clue he is sure of and pick up from there. The last clue in the series identifies the missing person. Clues such as the following are appropriate:

1. Look in the pocket of a book about stars by an author whose initials are H.A.R. (In the pocket of this book he will find the next clue.)
2. Look behind the title card for A.B. White's book about a spider. (The student will follow each clue in its turn until he reaches the last clue which will lead to the solution.)
3. The missing person for whom you are searching wrote a book whose call number is _____ .

Fact Finders—This is an individually run race against time. The student uses an atlas to find and record as many of the requested facts as he can in a given length of time. The following are some questions which can be answered by using Rand McNally's *Classroom Atlas*.

1. What is the area of Iceland?
2. What large city is located at approximately 35 S by 58 W?
3. What are the two major types of vegetation in India?
4. What is the population (to the nearest hundred) of Gibraltar?
5. When and how did the United States acquire Puerto Rico?

The extra preparation required for activities such as these can be shared by several teachers. If each of six teachers covering two or three grade levels prepared one of each of the five activities, a total of 30 multilevel activities would be available for use by all the classes.

Summary

This chapter has examined suggestions for differentiated activities in specific aspects of production and consumption of language. Differentiation in the spelling program can focus on selection of words to be learned, on methods to be employed and on rate of learning. The development of personalized styles of handwriting coupled with individualized practice to improve legibility, internal consistency and fluency allow for variation in handwriting instruction. Examples of differentiation of instruction in the mechanics of written expression included a discussion of a three-group plan based on the program in a grade level text and a description of a program utilizing packaged learning activities for independent study. Diversified methods of encouraging original writing and differing expectations for the finished products are two important components of the creative writing aspect of language production. Also important is provision for various ways of recognizing and sharing the written work. A discussion of alternatives in language consumption activities included suggestions for various ways to encourage enjoyment and sharing of literature and considered the provision of differentiated opportunities for practicing reference and library skills using game-like formats.

Capitalizing on Alternatives in Social Studies

_____ **8**

Our discussions dealing with reading and language arts have included a wide variety of suggestions and ideas drawn from many teachers. This chapter will deviate somewhat from the established format and will present in some detail a discussion of one teacher's plan for differentiating instruction in social studies for a fourth grade class of 32 students. Although the example considered here pertains to a specific grade level, the content of this program as well as its underlying principles relate to other grade levels as well. Within the framework of this one program, are a multitude of ideas which can be modified for use in any classroom without necessitating adoption of the total plan.

The students in this class covered a wide range of abilities, work habits and interests. Reading levels varied from one child at first grade level all the way up to two at junior high level. A few of the children were considered rather serious "behavior problems." The teacher was given copies of the state syllabus and the school district's curriculum guide for social studies, both calling for a study of famous Americans. On her bookshelves were ten or 12 copies of each of three social studies texts which were essentially collections of short biographies of American personalities arranged into units generally on the basis of historical periods in American history. The teacher also had several teachers' editions of other social studies texts, one globe and a wall map of the United States. The school library was well stocked and served as a media center as well as a book center. Audio-visual hardware and software were available for use in the library or in the classroom and school administrators were encouraging a multitext, multimedia approach to social studies instruction. In spite of some serious limitations in space and materials, the teacher felt that the overall situation was quite conducive to attempting a differentiated program.

PLANNING AND PREPARING FOR THE PROGRAM

Mrs. Stephen's first steps were in the nature of building a groundwork for her program. She wanted to establish a few basic guidelines and determine a general direction which would govern her own aims and efforts. Three areas of concern were identified. First, if requirements of the "course of study" as well as provision for differentiated instruction were to be accommodated, it would be essential to have a unifying, yet flexible framework around which to design the program. A definite plan for involving students in planning and taking part in learning activities was also felt to be an important aspect of the preparatory work. And, finally, it would be necessary to find, make, assemble or otherwise obtain such supplies and paraphernalia as would provide the raw materials for learning activities.

A Framework for Unity and Flexibility

An examination of the course of study outlined in the state syllabus and district curriculum guide revealed three major thrusts or goals of the program. One of these, in the realm of knowledge acquisition, was to develop an awareness of the role of immigrants and ethnic groups in the growth and development of the United States. Another was to increase ability in the use of map and globe skills. The third was to build attitudes leading to patriotic citizenship and an appreciation of American traditions and customs. The syllabus and curriculum guide defined several units of study which listed texts and other materials, discussion questions and learning activities and suggested specific content to be studied.

One of the first tangible steps to be taken by Mrs. Stephens was the development of a statement of general goals or objectives for students. These followed the three major thrusts of the program: knowledge, skills and attitudes.

Objectives relating to knowledge acquisition took the form of a list of five broad, general concepts which Mrs. Stephens felt gave specific direction and provided unity for the program, and at the same time allowed for considerable flexibility and individualization when it came to the selection of specifics for various children. See Figure 8-1.

Objectives relating to skill development emerged in the form of a simple outline.

I. Map and globe skills
   A. Latitude and longitude; hemispheres
   B. Map symbols
   C. Historical maps
   D. Special-purpose maps
II. Information-seeking skills
   A. Reference and trade books
   B. Library facilities
   C. Audio-visual media
III. Information-sharing skills
   A. Written
   B. Oral
   C. Visual
IV. Self-direction skills
   A. Setting objectives
   B. Planning and follow-through
   C. Self-evaluation

From this outline, it was a simple matter to identify the general direction to be followed in skill development activities. The degree of sophistication which an individual student might be expected to acquire and the specific activities in which he might engage were not rigidly defined. The desired flexibility was thus achieved without sacrificing overall unity.

Objectives relating to the building of patriotic attitudes and appreciation for traditions were stated in terms of general types of behavior or activity in which students could engage. Three such areas of behavior were identified.

1. Contribution to the celebration or recognition of national holidays and special events
2. Social involvement in the community
3. Physical involvement in community improvement

Again, the provision for flexibility within the scope of unifying direction has been maintained in the statement of these broad goals. Mrs. Stephens knew, in general, the area of expected activity for a child but had not definitively outlined specifics.

Mrs. Stephens visualized the statements of goals regarding knowledge and skills in the form of the two-dimensional grid shown in Figure 8-1. She felt that this model provided a structure which would govern the selection of learning opportunities for each child, making it possible to avoid aimless activities and confusion as to purpose. The desired flexibility was found in the freedom to hang upon this framework different specifics for different children. In other words, the way in which any given cell in the structure could be "filled up" and the selection of specific cells for attention might vary considerably from child to child. Thus a fairly individualized program could be built for each child, even though all members of the class would be working in some way toward the same general goals.

Matrix Framework for Goals Requiring
Knowledge Acquisition and Skill Development

Concepts	Map and Globe Skills	Info.-Seeking Skills	Info.-Sharing Skills	Self-Direction Skills
People from all over the world have come to live in our country throughout its history.				
Many groups and individuals have contributed to the growth and development of our country.				
The idea of the worth and rights of the individual has played an important role in the history of our country.				
Various ethnic groups have contributed to the development of our cultural and social traditions.				
The ideas and efforts of many leaders have contributed to the growth and development of our government, our educational system and other important institutions.				

Figure 8-1

A second approach to providing unity is found in the teacher's selection of six topics or areas of content to serve as focal points for classroom activities. These fell into two categories, with three topics having an historical or chronological orientation and the other three having a more general orientation. The historical topics followed the basic arrangement of the commercial texts and curriculum guide.

Discovery and Exploration
Colonial and Revolutionary War Periods
Establishment and Growth of our Nation

Topics in the general orientation category did not rely on chronology for internal organization. These dealt with specific types or areas of contributions to our country by various groups and individuals living here.

Customs, Traditions and Institutions in America
Contributions to Industry and Science
Contributions in Art and Sports

As a result of these planning efforts, Mrs. Stephens was able (1) to arrive at a framework of general goals which would give direction to the *kinds* of learning activities in which her students might engage, and (2) to identify several topics which would provide focal points for the *content* of the learning activities. The wide range of possibilities for specific activities which could fall within the framework of objectives and topics ensured Mrs. Stephens that she could provide for as much individualization as she felt able to handle.

The Student's Role

The second area of concern identified by Mrs. Stephens related to the role of the student in planning and carrying out his own learning activities. The concept of meaningful self-selection based upon the student's interiorized, though perhaps not verbalized, needs was felt to be a valid foundation on which to build this phase of the program. The children had previously had a limited amount of experience in decision making regarding their own learning activities. At the end of the year, they would move on to other teachers who might lean more heavily toward the spoon-feeding approach to instruction. Realizing that these factors of past and future expectations were a real part of the children's learning environment, Mrs. Stephens attempted to focus the student participation role on those activities which would contribute to achievement of the self-direction skills already identified as goals. Such skills would make a valuable contribution to good study habits in almost any situation.

Involvement in selecting from among alternative activities or types of activities and involvement in choosing specifics of content were felt to be two important aspects of the student's role in learning. As was mentioned earlier, part of Mrs. Stephens' plan for flexibility was found in the open-ended nature of the objectives. The value of this openendedness becomes apparent as we see how Mrs. Stephens lay the groundwork for student involvement in decision making and planning.

The Basic Groundwork

In order to make Mrs. Stephens' plan operative, it was first necessary to familiarize the students with the objectives of the program. A minimum of two weeks was earmarked for this purpose. Whole class, small group and individual activities were used. Differentiation in kinds and amounts of these introductory activities was necessary to insure adequate familiarity and understanding for all children. Typical of these introductory activities are the following examples:

●A large group discussion on the concept of *objectives* centered around two hypothetical situations likely to be experienced by all of the children at some time: "you are hungry" and "an aunt's birthday is approaching." The children decided that if you were hungry you would try to get something to eat, and that you might decide to give a gift to your aunt on her birthday. Expressions such as: something you want to get or do . . . like aiming at a target . . . a thing to try for . . . and reaching for a goal, were used interchangeably with the term objective.

●A bulletin board was started which listed pupil-composed definitions of the term objectives. In addition to this list were two illustrations, one of a boy who "looked hungry" and one of a calendar with a date circled in red and labeled "Aunt Betty's birthday."

●Small group brainstorming sessions approached the question of how do we reach our objectives. If you want something to eat, what are some of *the ways you can get* something to eat? If you want to give your aunt a birthday gift, what are some of the *ways* you can get her something?

●Other small group brainstorming sessions centered around the specific *things* you could get to eat or give to Aunt Betty.

●The bulletin board which started after the first discussion, was further developed as subsequent activities progressed. Ways of reaching objectives were listed horizontally under each illustration and specific examples for each of these methods arranged under the heading. See Figure 8-2 for a diagram of the bulletin board design.

Design of Bulletin Board on Objectives

Objectives: are _ _ _

Goals_ _ _ Targets_ _ _ Aims_ _ _

Reasons why_ _ _ Something to get _ _ _

What we want to do or have _ _ _ _

Things we try for_ _ _

Figure 8-2

●The notion of working for two objectives at the same time was handled in a large group discussion. Retaining the two original examples of getting something to eat and something for Aunt Betty's birthday, a further condition was introduced—the *thing* finally chosen to eat or to give must also be "good for" the person.

●Individually compiled lists were made and later shared with the whole class as an example of the many possible ways a person could decide to personally meet an objective. Each child was first asked to list five specific things he would choose to eat if he were hungry. Next he was asked to write the name of an aunt, sister, mother or grandmother, or female friend whom he might like to present with a special gift, and to list five things which he would like to give to that person. These five things must be within his personal range of possibility—a trip to the moon or a new automobile were out! The ultimate sharing of these lists offered the opportunity to discuss the many different ways specific children could reach the same goal.

●Small group sessions were held to discuss pupil reactions and suggestions to the lists of social studies objectives for the year. Wording of the objectives was simplified for use by students. Each of the three categories was handled separately. Discussions at this point were kept fairly general and were geared toward interpretation of the meanings of the objectives.

1. Here are some things (skills) that, by the end of this year, I hope you will be able to do better than you can do right now.

2. These are some "big ideas." By the end of the year, I hope you will be able to tell me quite a lot of information about some examples of each one.

3. This is a list of three kinds of things which you can do to help other people or to make our world a little better place to live. I hope that, by the end of the year, you will have done some of each kind of thing.

●The use of a matrix to show skills and knowledge objectives was introduced one step at a time by means of the overhead projector and an overlay transparency. The base transparency listed the five broad concepts in a lefthand column. Vertical strip overlays, one for each of the four major skill areas, could be shown one column at a time or in any desired combination until ultimately the entire four-by-five grid could be discussed. As each new skill strip was considered in isolation next to the list of broad concepts, or big ideas, children were asked to consider several activities and to decide in which space on the "chart" each "belonged." For example, *reading a book about George Washington* could be inserted next to concept number two under the information-seeking column; *drawing a map to show English, Spanish, French and Dutch colonies* would belong under map skills and next to concept number one; and *making a display about the Bill of Rights* might be placed next to either concept three or five in the information-sharing column. Children were also asked to suggest several possible kinds of activities that could be placed together in a designated space, or cell, on the grid. Suggestions for the concept four, information-seeking cell included such activities as reading about Halloween customs, seeing a movie about jazz music and looking for pictures of Christmas customs in other countries.

Four Phases of Expansion

Mrs. Stephens decided to use the first focal topic, Discovery and Exploration, as a kind of orientation unit. Her goal was to plan activities in this unit to serve a variety of exploratory and administrative purposes:

● To train the children in the use of various types of materials and in the keeping of specific records of progress,

● To give the teacher some insights into the *how much* and *how fast* aspects of independent study and self-direction for each pupil,

● To focus students' attentions on the self-direction skills objectives,

● To work gradually into as much self-selection, self-direction and independent study as seemed feasible, and

● To identify, and if possible to rectify, weaknesses and problems in her plan for differentiating instruction.

The branching out process assumed four phases. In the first of these, all children worked on the same specific goal, their self-selection being limited to a choice from among several alternative activities all aimed at a single purpose. For example, in the cell for map and globe skills for concept two, the following choices regarding historical maps were available. Children were to select and do any three.

1. Study a given map of John Cabot's explorations and answer ten questions about it.

2. Use any map or maps to answer six questions about Spanish explorations in North America, giving book title and page number for each map used.

3. Make a map showing (and labeling) Columbus' three trips to the Western Hemisphere, including his points of departure, his stops en route and his points of arrival back in Europe.

4. Study any map of French explorations in the New World and answer ten questions.

5. Make a map showing (and labeling) the explorations of any three of these men—Balboa, Marquette, Coronado, Hudson or Cabot.

6. Study as many maps as necessary to answer five questions about the age of exploration. Give the book title and page number for each map used.

The second phase of branching out called for each student to select the specific content for information seeking regarding the contribution made to America's history by any discoverer or explorer. This meant that each child selected a specific person to study, located appropriate sources of information and learned certain facts about him. Minimum standards for kinds of information were set, optional suggestions made and any additional pertinent facts accepted. Some training in use of library facilities, audio-visual materials and reference sources was undertaken. Also included in this activity was some preliminary work on the self-direction skills of planning and follow-through.

Phase three expanded the controlled branching out operation one more step. A specific cell on the grid of objectives was selected for this purpose—sharing information for concept one. Each child was to plan and do any activity relating to discovery and exploration which "fit into" this space on the grid. Additional guidance in self-direction skills was given in small group settings.

In the final phase of this part of the program, children were to select any specific objective, type of activity and specific content which fell within the grid of objectives and which related to the focal topic. At this point, Mrs. Stephens became aware of a significant weakness in her grid of objectives. There was no allowance made for skill development activities that did not relate directly to one of the five broad concepts. To remedy this, she simply added a sixth category in the concept column and labeled it "General Information."

Considerable small group instruction and individualized help in self-direction skill development was necessary throughout the branching out operation. Mrs. Stephens found that she had been too optimistic in her expectations. A large number of children required much teacher guidance. Altering her original plans, she decided to proceed more cautiously in this area, following the same basic four phases but taking smaller, slower steps toward significant independent study with all but a very few students.

Building Self-Contained Instructional Kits

Successful administration of a plan such as Mrs. Stephens' is significantly affected by the availability (or lack of it) of appropriate instructional materials. The third area of her planning and preparatory concerns centered around the selection, acquisition and arrangement of a wide range of types and levels of materials for use by her pupils in their learning activities. A survey of classroom and storeroom supplies and consultations with the school librarian and other classroom teachers revealed a surprisingly large assortment of materials already on hand in the building.

The discussion of her plans with the principal resulted in a modest amount of budget money being made available for the purchase of a few new materials for her classroom. In attempting to get the greatest mileage from the available sum, Mrs. Stephens decided to spend part of the money for materials to be used by children and part of it for raw materials for teacher-made items. She was able to purchase a dozen paperback classroom atlases, several assorted paperback biographies, three portfolios of loose pictures and pages of printed text on colonial Americans, pioneers and great Americans, several blank cassette tapes, a package of large sheets of oak tag and 300 acetate sheet protectors. (How would you spend $100?)

Using the six focal topics as unit categories, Mrs. Stephens assembled six sets of instructional materials. Each set contained three kits: a permanent kit, a supplementary kit and a circulating materials kit. In the permanent kits, she placed items which could remain in her classroom all year and from year to year. Supplemental kits were assembled as each new unit was introduced to the class and contained materials on six weeks' loan from the school and public libraries, from other teachers and from pupils. Materials which were available only on short term loan—films, filmstrips, certain reference books and exhibits from museums and art galleries—were placed in the circulating materials kit with constant turnover geared to the progress of the unit under study. Of the three kits in a given set, the permanent kit was the nerve center for all activities relating to that unit of study.

Contents of permanent kits were gleaned from materials assigned to and purchased for the classroom, from contributions from parents, teachers and from any other available source, and from Mrs. Stephens' own store of instructional items. Also included was a wide assortment of teacher-made materials. Catalogs listing sources of free and inexpensive materials were valuable assets for the acquisition of new materials. A typical permanent kit contained the following types of ready-made materials:

> books—including classroom social studies books and discards from school and public libraries
>
> maps
>
> paperbacks
>
> slides
>
> pictures
>
> charts
>
> articles and short stories—clipped from magazines and old social studies or reading books and protected by oak tag covers or acetate sheet protectors
>
> looseleaf pictures and related text pages—selected from portfolios mentioned earlier.

Teacher-made materials came from three sources. Selections were made from among Mrs. Stephens' files of previously used worksheets, map exercises and game type activities. Several other teachers contributed copies of materials they had made. However, most teacher-made materials were designed and prepared especially for the kits. Of the new materials, many were the result of a summer project. Others were added during the course of the school year. An attempt was made to add at least one significant contribution to one of the kits each week.

Short term paper-and-pencil activities included several types of materials. Introductory, or "teaching," lessons were generally prepared at more than one level of difficulty. The same was true of practice materials, worksheets and study guides. A variety of teacher-made tests was included: some for students' self-evaluation, others for teacher evaluation. Many overview activities were presented as games or brainteasers, such as crossword puzzles, riddles and word searches. An example of a short term activity is shown in Figure 8-3.

The heading on this activity indicates the permanent kit from which it was taken, the place in the kit where it should be returned and the specific objectives to which it relates. This method of identification was used on all materials in the permanent kits except when specific objectives were not identified for multipurpose or generalized items such as atlases, texts, many paperbacks and certain games.

ARTS AND SPORTS

General Practice: Arts 5–B

Objectives: Concept 2
               Information Seeking and Information Sharing
Part I.   Use your information-seeking skills to help you complete
               the following table of information about five artists.

Name of Artist	Type of Art Work	Special Style	Title or Name of 1 Work	Special Comment
Jackson Pollock				
Frank Lloyd Wright				
John Marin				
Alexander Calder				
Piet Mondrian				

Part II.   Look at the art prints in the attached envelope. Select one
               which interests you. Read the information about the artist
               on the back of the print. Write a short report telling
               (a) about the artist, (b) about this particular art work, and
               (c) why this particular one interested you.

Figure 8-3

Teacher-made materials also related to longer investigation and project activities. Each kit contained classroom quantities of a list of suggested project ideas. Children were encouraged to add new ideas to the master list and undertake projects other than those listed. Several typical suggestions drawn from various kits are listed here as illustrations of the type of project ideas which could be used in this manner. The specific kit and objectives are identified for each.

●Make a series of dioramas or transparencies which tells the story of one of the following: Lewis and Clark, Daniel Boone, Marcus and Narcissa Whitman, Bill Cody or Sam Houston.

Establishing and Building Our Nation
Concept 2, Information Sharing and Self-Direction

●Draw a time line about American astronauts and events in our explorations of space.

> Science and Industry
> Concept 2, Information Sharing
> and Self-Direction

●Do a bulletin board about one of the following: Where Our Christmas Customs Got Started; Special Religious Holidays; Folk Dances; The History of Halloween; Spirituals, Jazz and Soul Music; or Early American Parties and Festivals.

> Customs, Traditions and Institutions
> Concept 4, Information Seeking
> and Sharing, Self-Direction

●Make an exhibit of pictures and interesting facts for one of these titles: Baseball Hall of Fame, Football Hall of Fame, Racing Hall of Fame, etc.

> Arts and Sports
> Concept 2, Information Sharing
> and Self-Direction

●Make a "filmstrip" (on a long roll of paper) or a "comic book" story about the inventions or discoveries of one of the following: Benjamin Franklin, Thomas Edison, Alexander Graham Bell, Wright brothers, Eli Whitney or Samuel Morse.

> Science and Industry
> Concept 2, Information Seeking
> and Sharing, Self-Direction

●Plan an oral report about U.S. postage stamps that honor famous men studied in this unit. Make a tape recording of your report. If possible make an exhibit of some of these stamps or pictures of them and pictures of some of the men honored on the postage stamps.

> Appropriate for all kits and
> various concepts, Information
> Seeking and Sharing, Self-
> Direction

●Prepare a series of historical maps showing locations of important events in famous men's lives, during the time just before and during the American Revolution

> Colonial and Revolutionary War
> Periods
> Concepts 1, 2, Map and Globe
> Skills, Self-Direction

Long term activities also included investigation projects which were administered with the aid of project guides. These were designed to provide practice in using a wide variety of reference materials and library facilities. Many options were available both in choice of specific topics for investigation and in the scope and depth of investigations to be undertaken. Some stipulations about minimum requirements and acceptable standards were generally included.

Several other types of teacher-made materials completed the collection in the permanent kit. Introductory or teaching lessons were often recorded on cassette tapes to be used in conjunction with some referent such as a set of maps, worksheets, overhead transparencies, slides or pictures. Forms for record keeping were designed for use by pupils as well as by the teacher. A *Source of Resources* list included information about specific kinds of materials available in the library relating to the focal topic of the kit. A *Student's Unit Guide* contained an overview of the materials and activities contained in the three types of unit kits and a statement of minimum required work and suggested options.

A packet of teacher reference materials assisted Mrs. Stephens in the administration of the unit. Lists of materials for permanent, supplemental and circulating materials kits were included in this packet. Also included were samples of all materials to be used by students, evaluation devices, record keeping forms and pupil conference guides. Ideas for additional activities and for teacher-led small or large group sessions were added to the packet as inspiration and need arose.

Mrs. Stephens' planning and preparatory work provided her with a unifying, yet flexible framework for differentiating the social studies program to meet the varying levels, rates and interests of her pupils. Provisions for student involvement characterized all phases of planning and preparation. The sets of instructional kits organized available materials and made them easily accessible to students and teacher. This advance planning and preparation contributed to the smooth administration of the program and to the overall sense of direction and purpose which was to be found even in the midst of very diverse activities.

THE PLAN IN OPERATION

Due to considerations of classroom organization and space limitations, Mrs. Stephens arbitrarily assigned a six weeks' block of time to each unit. The first few days of each were devoted largely to whole class sessions. These sessions were held for the purpose of presenting a general overview of the unit and to allow for a period of generalized planning.

The unit overview consisted of three aspects. The first of these dealt with unit content and provided an introduction to the historical period or the scope of the focal topic to be studied. Films or filmstrips, whole class discussions and study of Source of Resources lists and lists of suggested activities for the unit assisted in this aspect of the overview. Also included in the overview were activities aimed at making students aware of specific objectives stressed in the unit. Although each unit dealt to some extent with all objectives, certain units were more conducive than others to a concentration on one or more objective. With regard to skills, for example, the units on Discovery and Exploration and Colonial and Revolutionary War Periods provided a wealth of opportunities to work with map and globe skills. Emphasis in the next two units was placed upon skills of information seeking and sharing. Self-direction skills were most strongly stressed in the last two units. The third aspect of the unit overview was planned to acquaint students with specific items to be found in the three kits of instructional materials.

Whole class planning was restricted to generalized concerns. Some of these included establishing a tentative schedule of deadlines and special events, deciding on the general approach to scheduling study time for pursuing various activities and determining the nature of the "finale" or whole-class culminating activity. A discussion of pitfalls experienced in the previous unit regarding deadlines and study times and conditions were helpful. Also of general concern were plans for any major large group projects or special holiday events.

After the first exploratory and orientation sessions, activities became somewhat more differentiated. Approximately two weeks would be devoted to small group sessions and individual pursuit of required short term activities. The small group sessions focused on teacher guidance in planning for lengthier projects and in the introduction of new aspects of skill development. As a student became more adept at organizing and carrying out his own plans, he was included in fewer of the teacher-led small group sessions. Weekly discussions with the entire class were held to assess general progress and to make any desirable changes in the original schedule and overall plan. Gradually more and more of the students were able to work independently for longer periods of time. A few never reached the point where they could be productive without some form of teacher guidance or contact daily.

Arrangements had been made with the library-media center for daily periods of time during which students could use A-V equipment and software in the library. Specific sessions were scheduled with the librarian to train children in the use of a particular type of reference material or specific library facility. Whether or not a given child was required to attend a session depended upon that child's demonstrated skill in the use of the material or facility to be focused upon.

With the cooperation of the librarian, an experiment was conducted during the course of one unit of study. One of the school's circulating filmstrip projectors and one of the tape cassettes with a six-position listening post were "stored" in Mrs. Stephens' room when not requested for use in another classroom. Since there were other circulating projectors and cassettes, the demand for those kept in her classroom was not excessive. Sometimes several days would pass without a request for this equipment. By using her room as an annex to the A-V storeroom, Mrs. Stephens was able to provide her class with the projector and listening center for better than half of the time. The convenience of having the equipment available so much of the time more than compensated for the inconvenience of delivery to and pick-up from other classrooms. A daily check of the sign-up sheet for this A-V equipment or a call on the intercom from the library would result in delivery of the requested item to the proper classroom by one of Mrs. Stephens' students. A team of four students was responsible for this task. The experiment worked satisfactorily for the six weeks' period, and the librarian was willing to continue it as long as it did not become too cumbersome to administer. Thus, in an informal way, the arrangement was made "tentatively permanent" for the second half of the year and contributed greatly to the program.

A Three-Ring Circus

As the six weeks' period progressed, students increasingly turned their attention to long term projects, and the classroom atmosphere took on some of the aspects of a three-ring circus. If you have ever attended a three-ring circus, you may recall how such a scene at first appears to be a flurry of unorganized confusion with all performers doing something different at the same time. The observer can make little sense out of the whole thing, but as he begins to attend to one center of activity at a time he can see that each performer has his own appointed place and task in the overall mosaic. So it was during many of Mrs. Stephens' social studies "periods"—an overall picture of diversified activity, which, to the casual glance, might at first have seemed unorganized, but which, on closer observation, revealed a collection of individuals or small groups of students purposefully pursuing many diversified tasks of the moment. At some given point in time, all of the following activities could have been going on simultaneously:

Eight students in library

- Four working with librarian on required guided practice in using the card catalog.
- One tracking down a film on the Bill of Rights.
- One previewing a filmstrip looking for information on Freedom of Speech.
- Two at the study table taking notes for reports on The History of Texas and the Gold Rush.

Small group activities in classroom

- Three students working with teacher receiving individualized help in planning long term projects.
- Two children cutting out letters and mounting illustrations for a bulletin board on Missionaries in the West.
- Four students at the listening center hearing a dramatization about the Constitutional Convention.

Individual activities in classroom

- Reading biographies
- Copying a written report on The Oregon Territory
- Using filmstrip projector to copy illustration from filmstrip on The Louisiana Purchase
- Drawing a map of the Lewis and Clark Expedition
- Taking a self-administered test on reference skills stressed in the unit
- Making a model of a covered wagon
- Doing a required short term exercise on Using an Index
- Completing an optional worksheet based on reading tables of information
- Creating a shoebox diorama about the Pony Express
- Making a series of maps on the Growth of the U.S. after 1800

Each of these activities would have been part of an overall series of activities to be pursued during the course of the unit of study. Many were part of required projects. Others were optional or extra activities which the students elected to do. Most of the activities were guided to some extent by the Unit Guide and/or one of the Project Guides found in the permanent kit for this unit. At the same time, most of the activities provided options for choices in either the content of the project or the type of project to be undertaken.

The Class Museum

One of the ongoing features of this social studies program was a class museum. Portions of the bulletin board, counter and bookshelves which stretched across the back of the room were set aside to serve as the setting for the museum. Here were arranged finished projects, displays and exhibits prepared by the students or brought in from the local museum or art gallery on short term loan. Student projects were displayed for at least one week, after which they were removed as needed to make room for newly completed exhibits. As displays were retired from the museum, they were stored elsewhere in the room to be used later as part of the culmination of the unit.

At the end of the first unit studied, each pupil was asked to select one visual project he had made during the unit. These selections were to be exhibited "publicly" for the rest of the school to enjoy. Hallway space outside the classroom was designated for this purpose. Three work sessions were devoted to the planning, preparation and setting up of the museum displays. The major problem to be overcome was how to place all the exhibits on or very close to the walls in the hallway. Three-dimensional exhibits were especially difficult to manage. Orange crates, concrete blocks and wooden planks were used to create display areas which were placed along the walls so as to occupy a minimum of the passageway. The children designed notices about the museum and delivered these to all classrooms in the building. During the two-day exhibit, many classes came to view the displays and a few sent thank you notes to the class.

The general feeling among the children in Mrs. Stephens' class was that a public sharing of the class museum should be planned for the end of each unit. Several improvements were considered necessary for subsequent exhibits. A better place to hold the exhibit was highly desirable. If possible, a longer showing time was also recommended, as well as better, more interesting ways of displaying projects.

The second public showing of the class museum was held in the entrance foyer and main office. More time and thought were devoted to display and arrangement techniques and equipment. Cardboard carpentry constructions, multifold floor screens and free-standing room divider screens were added to the original display facilities. Paint, crepe paper, colored burlap and fabric contributions were used to make the backgrounds more attractive. The art teacher was asked to advise and suggest during the planning and setting-up of the exhibit. All of these factors resulted in a much more satisfactory exhibit and the museum remained on display for two weeks.

Subsequent museum exhibits were held on the stage, in the library and in the cafeteria. The final museum of the year was set up in the classroom on one day and was followed by an "open house" the next day. All classes in the school were scheduled for the open house, and parents of Mrs. Stephens' pupils were invited. Each new location of the museum presented unique considerations of space and traffic flow. Continued consultation with the art teacher, books on display techniques from the public library and class trips to the art gallery and museum resulted in increased sophistication in arranging and displaying the exhibits. Knowledge that the exhibits would be on public display also increased motivation to produce thorough, accurate and visually pleasing projects with the result that the quality of these increased as the year progressed.

Service to Others

Three general objectives of this social studies program did not appear on the objectives grid. These were the objectives relating to observation of national holidays and to social and physical involvement in the community. Social and physical involvement was approached through a Service to Others Project which turned out to be, in effect, a series of projects. These ranged in duration from one day to all year. A few were whole class projects, while others were carried out by only one or a few of the children. None were mandatory.

The Service to Others Project was treated as part of the overall social studies program but was considered separately from the regular units of study. Weekly sessions were devoted to discussion and planning of service activities. The project at first focused upon services which could be rendered in the home and at school. Gradually the scope was expanded to include the larger community.

To qualify as a Service to Others, an activity must be aimed at improving some specific situation or condition for someone other than the student, must be done without any tangible reward or remuneration and must be a voluntary act. Most of these activities were a matter of classwide discussion and planning, but occasionally a child would elect to perform a service which he did not wish to tell others about. This was not discouraged. Any such private projects could be discussed in a confidential conference with the teacher or could be kept strictly a personal matter. Examples of Service to Others Activities are described briefly below.

Individual Activities

●Weekly visits to an invalid neighbor. . .

●Mowing lawn for neighbor whose lawn mower was temporarily out of order. . .

●Watering houseplants for an aunt while she was away on vacation. . .

●Entertaining a neighbor's preschool youngster for an hour each afternoon after school for two weeks while the mother, who was recuperating from an illness, rested. . .

●Helping parents with extra chores around the house or yard. . .

●Serving as a teacher's aide before and after school for a first grade teacher. . .

●Using branches trimmed from the family's Christmas tree to make holiday door sprays for two elderly neighbors who lived alone. . .

●Tape recording stories to share with blind residents of the County Home and with students in a nearby sight saving class. . .

Small Group Activities

●Serving as kindergarten helpers by assisting kindergarten teachers in getting children ready to go home or at special, pre-arranged times during the day. . .

●Several "beautify the school" projects, including planting and maintaining a flower bed near the main entry, a dish garden in the library, holiday decorations in the cafeteria, a mini-art gallery in the nurse's office. . .

●Cleaning up a neighborhood eye-sore by removing debris from a vacant lot. . .

●Making and distributing to elderly, ill or otherwise likely neighbors several old-fashioned May baskets. . .

●Establishing a nurse's aide program, with students "on call" to assist nurse with errands, paperwork, picking up, gathering coats, etc. for ill youngsters who were going to be sent home, or any other necessary task. . .

●Reading stories aloud to kindergarten, first and second grade students by prearrangement with teachers or librarian. . .

Whole Class Activities

● Participating in Junior Red Cross projects such as assembling overseas boxes. . .

● Making tray favors and room decorations for residents of the County Home. . .

• Preparing "entertainment boxes" for schoolmates from any classroom who were hospitalized or at home for long periods. . . (Entertainment boxes included age-appropriate items, such as pictures to color, drawing paper, student-made booklets and stories to read, crossword puzzles, mazes, dot-to-dot activities, "fun" dittos, pages of jokes and riddles, old children's magazines and toys donated for this purpose.)

• Policing the school grounds, picking up papers and debris, from time to time, as the need seemed apparent. . .

• Taking part in a one-to-one project which involved each student's performing secret services for one special person whom the student felt could use a little extra "sunshine" in his life and whose identity the student did not reveal to anyone. . .

Holiday Specials

The objective calling for contributions to the celebration or recognition of national holidays and special events was approached by several specific projects dealing with selected national "happenings." National holidays, especially those honoring famous Americans or events in American history, and special recognition days or weeks, were chosen to serve as focal points for classroom activities. Student committees were established to plan and organize specific events for each holiday.

The amount of student participation in this aspect of the program varied considerably. Each student was asked to serve on at least one holiday committee during the year. Interested students were permitted to serve on additional committees. Nearly all holiday projects offered some type of opportunity for voluntary participation or contributions. Some students made contributions or took part in nearly all projects. Others contributed the minimum of time and effort.

Although each committee was given a standard task, the planning and organizing of specific events for a holiday, there was considerable variety in approach and outcome. Teacher guidance varied in quantity and quality according to the needs of the specific group. One or two groups required almost daily teacher-led sessions in order to achieve the goal. Others required little more than a brief conference with the teacher to define overall plans and schedules. The wide variety of resulting events illustrates the varying degrees of creativity and enthusiasm expressed by the student committees.

The Columbus Day committee presented a program featuring a recorded dramatization of the story of Christopher Columbus, accompanied by a series of colored transparency illustrations made by the committee and correlated with the script of the recorded story. Oral readings of a few poems about Columbus were followed by the distribution of copies of the poems and several "fun" dittos featuring the Columbus theme which students assembled into activity booklets to use in school or take home as they wished. Subsequent holiday specials featured similar programs utilizing films, filmstrips, student dramatizations and exhibits.

A bulletin board was always included in the plans for a holiday special. A few of these were made solely by the committee but most were open to contributions from the whole class. This was one of the most popular options elected by the students who made frequent contributions. On one occasion the committee arranged to have the art teacher work with the class on a large mural. During February the art teacher supervised construction of dioramas depicting events in the lives of George Washington and Abraham Lincoln. A sing-along program of patriotic songs led by the music teacher was part of a pre-Fourth-of-July celebration held in June.

A series of projects marked the recognition of American Education Week. Small desk bouquets were made and delivered to all teachers on Teacher Recognition Day. Other events of the week included slides and pictures of early American schools, a mock session of early American "lessons" using copies of excerpts from very old schoolbooks and a packet of fun dittos entitled School Daze. The last day of the week was designated as Be Kind to Mrs. Stephens Day and was highlighted by a program of skits, songs and poems on the school theme, followed by refreshments.

Keeping Track of Student Progress

Administering a diversified and differentiated program such as the one discussed here presents unique problems in the matter of keeping track of student progress. The traditional class register and grade book is inadequate for this purpose. Here it is necessary to know which activities each pupil has engaged in, what his long range plans are and which projects he is working on. The teacher must also be aware of the quality of the student's work as compared with realistic expectations for him and of the kinds of thinking and learning that are taking place in his experience. This kind of record keeping requires much more than a daily or weekly numerical or letter grade entered next to his name and averaged at the end of a reporting period to yield a report card grade.

Mrs. Stephens found that her grid of objectives could be adapted to serve two record keeping needs. Each child was given a copy of the grid for each of the six units. He used this to record notations of activities he engaged in during the unit of study. This presented him with a visual reminder of objectives which might still need attention as a unit progressed and gave him a tangible overview of the work he had accomplished. A large-scale model of the grid was also mounted on the classroom wall. This grid had a class list posted in each cell. Here Mrs. Stephens entered information about projects and activities undertaken by each student. A notation in pencil indicated that an activity had been started. The notation was retraced with color when the project was completed. This large chart presented an instant picture of the direction of individual and total class activity.

A three-ring loose-leaf notebook was set up to serve three record keeping purposes. At the front was a Teacher's Daily Log where Mrs. Stephens wrote notations, comments and anecdotes regarding pupil activities and regarding the general administration of the program. Some of this data was subsequently entered on Pupil Data Sheets. One of these data sheets for each child was found alphabetically arranged in the center section of the notebook. Here a running account of pupil progress was kept together with teacher comments and suggestions for future activities. The last section in the notebook contained Class Data Sheets. These were charts for recording raw scores earned by students on required worksheets, evaluation instruments and other teacher-scored activities.

A file folder for each child was also maintained. Pupil Data Sheets and Pupil-Teacher Conference Sheets were placed here as they were completed. Samples of student work were also kept on file. Most of these were returned to the student after the termination of the unit. Some student work was kept for comparison purposes later in the year or for use in parent-teacher conferences.

These three record keeping devices—the wall chart, the loose-leaf notebook and the file folders—provided a fairly comprehensive ongoing record of student progress. Additional short term records were utilized from time to time for specific purposes when more detailed information was required.

Summary

This chapter discusses in considerable detail one plan for providing alternatives in the social studies program. A desire for a flexible plan containing unity of purpose and direction resulted in the construction of a framework matrix of knowledge acquisition objectives and skill development objectives and in the identification of six very broad focal topics for units of study. Provisions were made for the student's active involvement in planning and selecting specific kinds and contents of learning activities within the program's overall framework. A third aspect of planning and preparing for this differentiated program centered around the construction of kits of instructional materials and learning activity guides to serve as the nerve center for the program's administration.

A discussion of the plan in operation points to the use of orientation and generalized planning sessions as introductory activities for each unit followed by increasingly diverse and self-directed activities of both short and long duration. A class museum served as an ongoing feature of the program and contributed a focus for certain culminating activities for the units. Objectives relating to involvement in service to others were approached through a variety of individual, small group and whole class service projects. Contributions to patriotic events centered around committee-planned observances of national holidays. Consideration was also given to the problems of record keeping and student progress in a program of diversified activities such as this one.

Building a Differentiated Arithmetic Program

— 9

For years controversy has existed over the concept of a child-centered approach as opposed to a subject-centered approach to curriculum building. Such a controversy seems to assume that the two approaches must be mutually exclusive. But is this truly the way it is? Wouldn't it be possible to build an instructional program which takes into consideration both the logical development of the child and the logical development of the subject? This chapter is based on the assumption that it is not only possible but highly desirable to design instruction in arithmetic with just such a child/subject orientation. Since much of the commercially available instructional material for elementary school arithmetic is already developed on the basis of the logic of the discipline, we will consider ways in which to incorporate child-oriented modifications into such a program.

ADJUSTING SCOPE AND SEQUENCE

The total scope and sequence of elementary school arithmetic skills and concepts have been broken down into six or seven grade level "packages" by most published programs. These packages generally come to the teacher in the form of a textbook sometimes accompanied by a workbook and occasionally supplemented by some sort of instructional aids ranging from ditto exercises for extra practice to various kinds of concrete manipulative materials.

A chart is frequently used to visually illustrate the overall scope of the program and the sequential development of skills and concepts within a grade level as well as throughout the program. A spiraling design is often employed in the building of the program. Essentially this means that a child moving through the program will be exposed to a given skill area (such as addition of whole numbers) periodically throughout the program, enabling him to review and extend his ability to understand and use the subskills and concepts related to that area. The scope and sequence chart and the spiral program design are components which can prove useful to the teacher planning to incorporate child-oriented modifications in a grade level program.

Many of the published arithmetic series are designed with various means for differentiating instruction to some extent. This may mean that provision has been made for the involvement of children in certain manipulative activities. It could also mean that some extra pages (or extra suggestions) have been provided for the child who needs additional practice or for the child who could handle some enrichment activities. A careful analysis of characteristics such as these will give the teacher some idea of the extent to which a given program has built-in opportunities for child-oriented modifications. Take advantage of these opportunities if they are there, but do not limit yourself to them. And remember that in your third grade class you probably don't have one single child who could qualify in every respect as a typical third grader, not even as a typical third-grade arithmetic student.

Establishing Priorities Regarding Scope

A typical second grade math text may contain units of study on such topics as Sets, Numbers and Numeration, Place Value, Geometry, Fractions and Measurement, as well as on the four basic computational skill areas of addition, subtraction, multiplication and division of whole numbers. A close look at the contents of the units contained in any grade level text will convince the teacher that not all of the children in her class will be able to cover all of the expected material with even a minimum degree of understanding and competence. In such cases, the teacher is called upon to make a decision about scope and rate. Will she usher the class through the program at a rate which will enable all the children to "finish" the book in one year thus implying acceptance of the high degree of confusion, frustration and failure attendant upon this arbitrary pacing, or will she modify the scope of the program to accommodate slower learning rates and lower readiness levels for some children and higher rates and levels for others? Those electing the latter option are faced with a decision about how to modify the scope of the program to allow for differentiated "coverage."

Three of the many possible methods for approaching scope modification for a given grade level text will be discussed briefly. We will use the hypothetical second grade program mentioned above to illustrate these approaches.

The first method is perhaps the one most commonly followed by teachers. Here all children are started at the beginning of the text and progress as one or more groups through as much of the book as can comfortably be handled by most of the children in the group. Thus the scope of the program for these children is determined by the sequence of the text and a rate of progress which accommodates the majority of the children in the group. This method does little toward meeting the widely varied rates and abilities found in most classes but it is one step better than hurrying all children through the whole book.

A second method calls for classifying the topics or units of instruction into three priority groupings. One group would contain those units, or parts of units, considered essential for minimum developmental coverage. Another group would consist of all those portions of the second grade program except those which the teacher feels could easily be postponed until another year when the built-in spiraling effect of the total program would again deal with these topics. The third group would consist of the entire program contained in the text. Of the many possible groupings, one is given here as an illustration, but not necessarily as a recommendation. Asterisks indicate units or parts of units not included in the previous grouping.

Group I (Minimal)
Addition
Subtraction
Place Value
Measurement
(part of)
Fractions

Group II
* (part of) Sets
* (part of) Numbers and Numeration
Addition
Subtraction
Place Value
* Multiplication
* (part of) Division
Measurement
* Fractions (all)

Group III
* * Sets (all)
* * Number and Numeration (all)
*   Addition
*   Subtraction
*   Place Value
*   Multiplication
* * Division (all)
*   Measurement
*   Fractions
* * Geometry

The third method for modifying scope is similar to the second except that it implies a more highly individualized pattern of progress than the second. The second method, as described above, lends itself readily to a three-group approach to instruction, although it, too, can be more individualized if desired. The third method, discussed below, almost requires considerable individualization.

Here, the units of study are grouped in a single list arranged according to priority. Certain units lend themselves to subdivision. For example, a typical addition unit may be broken down into three subunits of (1) the basic addition facts, (2) simple column addition and word problems and (3) column addition and word problems involving regrouping. In such cases, the subunits may not receive the same priority rating and may not be listed contiguously. The plan would be to have individual or small groups of children follow this continuum of arithmetic topics at a comfortable rate of continuous progress. Some provision for flexibility in sequence would be desirable, with the greater amount of latitude for the more able and more rapid learners. With this method, scope is again determined by sequence and rate, but sequence is established by the teacher and is not as rigid as in the first method, and greater provision is made for progressing at individual and widely varying rates.

Providing Flexibility in Sequence

The arrangement of arithmetic skills and concepts into a given sequence appears to be based partly on the logic of the discipline, partly on tradition and partly on arbitrary decisions.

Subtraction is *related* to addition, being the inverse operation of addition; therefore, instruction in subtraction generally follows that in addition or is taught in conjunction with it. However, there is also a relationship between addition and multiplication which could be used as a rationale for placing instruction in multiplication immediately after addition. Teachers have often noted an interesting phenomenon with regard to children's patterns of success in the four operations of addition, subtraction, multiplication and division; namely, that many children show great success with addition and multiplication but little success with subtraction and division. Perhaps for these children a change in sequence of instruction from the traditional one to one based on success experiences would be desirable.

Often in arithmetic, understanding of one kind is a prerequisite for understanding of another kind. For example, an understanding of the rudiments of place value in the decimal system is necessary for an understanding of the process of regrouping in addition or subtraction. If *understanding* is one of the objectives to be considered in a unit on regrouping in addition or subtraction, then flexibility in the sequential placement of instruction in place value is limited. It must come sometime prior to the unit on regrouping.

However, some children can achieve a certain degreee of success in computations involving regrouping even without an understanding of place value, but their success is based on a rote memorization of the algorithms involved and not on real understanding. Still other children achieve an understanding of place value through inference and do not need special instruction in it. Thus such factors as prerequisite skills, specific instructional objectives and awareness of individual children's already existing understandings affect decisions about sequence flexibility.

One way to organize your own thinking about flexibility in sequence for arithmetic instruction is to develop some kind of visual device which shows at a glance where the options for flexibility lie and where prerequisite skills and/or understandings limit flexibility. Figure 9-1 illustrates one possible way to do this. The examples given are drawn from the four areas of addition, subtraction, multiplication and division of whole numbers and are not all-inclusive even there. On the right-hand vertical column are listed subskills where flexibility in sequence would be possible. When prerequisite skills and understandings are called for, these are listed horizontally to the left of the dark line.

Thus you can see that while in some cases flexibility is limited, in others it is extensive. Flexibility in deciding when to work with "long division" would be limited to some time *after* acquisition of prerequisite skills and understandings in subtraction facts, multiplication facts, division facts, place value, subtraction with regrouping and multiplication with regrouping. On the other hand, a child could conceivably proceed far down the list of addition and multiplication

OPTIONS FOR FLEXIBILITY IN SEQUENCING

Prerequisites	Subskill Areas
	Addition facts
	Subtraction facts
	Multiplication facts
	Division facts
Addition facts	2- & 3-digit column addition, no regrouping
Subtraction facts	2- & 3-digit subtraction, no regrouping
Multiplication facts	2- & 3-digit multiplication by 1 digit, no regrouping
Division facts	2- & 3-digit division by 1 digit, no regrouping
	Place value, to 3 places
Addition facts, place value	2- & 3-digit column addition with regrouping
Subtraction facts, place value	2- & 3-digit subtraction with regrouping
Addition with regrouping, multiplication no re-grouping	2- & 3-digit multiplication by 1 digit, with regrouping
Multiplication facts, division facts, subtraction with regrouping	2- & 3-digit division by 1 digit, with regrouping
Multiplication by 1 digit with regrouping	2- & 3-digit multiplication by 2 digit, with regrouping
Division by 1 digit with regrouping	2- & 3-digit division by 2 digits, with regrouping

Figure 9-1

subskills without ever having been involved in subtraction or division. He cannot go very far down the list, however, without some understanding of place value.

ADAPTING TECHNIQUES TO LEARNING RATES AND STYLES

Much is said in education today about learning modalities. Without becoming highly involved and technical, we can recognize that all children do not learn the same way, nor does a given child learn best with a single method or set of methods at all times. Learning more about how each of our students learns gives us another avenue by which to introduce child-oriented modifications into our arithmetic programs.

A first step in adapting instructional methods and techniques to take advantage of individual styles and rates is the evaluation of each student's patterns of learning and habits of study. One way to do this is to use a checklist or rating scale which is updated periodically for each child. An example of such a rating scale is given in Figure 9-2.

EVALUATION OF LEARNING STYLES IN ARITHMETIC

	Low —— *High*
1. Need for concrete manipulative activities	1 2 3 4 5
2. Need for audio-visual teacher demonstrations	1 2 3 4 5
3. Need for teacher direction and supervision	1 2 3 4 5
4. Need for drill and practice activities	1 2 3 4 5
5. Need for review and maintenance activities	1 2 3 4 5
6. Ability to comprehend arithmetic text	1 2 3 4 5
7. Can move rapidly to paper-and-pencil activities	1 2 3 4 5
8. Works well independently	1 2 3 4 5
9. Works well with other students	1 2 3 4 5
10. Learns inductively	1 2 3 4 5
11. Learns deductively	1 2 3 4 5
12. Attention span	1 2 3 4 5
13. Interest and motivation in arithmetic	1 2 3 4 5
14. Benefits from interest center and game activities	1 2 3 4 5
15. Follows oral directions	1 2 3 4 5
16. Follows written directions	1 2 3 4 5
17. Completes homework assignments	1 2 3 4 5
18. Learns from correcting own errors	1 2 3 4 5
19. Perseveres with reasonable tasks	1 2 3 4 5
20. Tolerance for frustration	1 2 3 4 5

Figure 9-2

An analysis of a pupil's standing on this evaluation device enables the teacher to determine types and amounts of introductory, practice and extension activities for that child. For example, students rating high on the first five items will require much teacher-led and supervised activity and will probably move rather slowly in the arithmetic program. Pupils rating high in most of the remaining items will be likely candidates for considerable independent and self-directed activity. Most children in a class will probably benefit from teacher-led activities part of the time and from independent or pupil-team activities at other times, depending upon the purpose of the specific activity.

Teacher-Led Sessions

Teacher-led activities can serve a variety of purposes. Certain types of pupil evaluation are best done in teacher-led sessions because of ease of administration, need for controlled environment or desirability of firsthand observation of pupils during performance of specific tasks. Introductory, orientation and training activities are often effectively and efficiently handled in teacher-directed sessions. Developmental activities and practice exercises may frequently call for teacher-led lessons especially with children needing considerable guidance and supervision. Teacher-supervised and -directed activities can be planned for small groups as well as for the whole class, and for part of a lesson as well as for an entire period. This increases the flexibility of the teacher-led session as an instructional method.

Children requiring the greatest amount of teacher-led activity will be those rating high on the first five items of the Evaluation of Learning Styles Instrument. Teacher demonstrations, illustrative material, manipulative activities, step-by-step directed practice with immediate feedback and constantly available teacher assistance are important factors to consider in planning for these children. You may find it helpful to have several sets of each of several types of concrete materials for use in teacher-led small group sessions. Listed below are some suggested types of manipulative materials which can be used in various ways in such teacher-directed activities.

● Counters, such as blocks, discs, pebbles, buttons, paper clips, etc.

● Models of our number system such as ᴿ Cuisennaire Rods or similar modular devices.

● Play money (sets with pennies, dimes and dollars are especially helpful in working with place value).

●Numerical anagrams with signs for addition, subtraction, multiplication, division, equality, inequality, union or intersection of sets, etc. as needed. Children can make their own sets with oak tag cards and felt pens.

●Fraction pies and/or fraction pieces where congruent circles or long rectangles in different colors are cut into fractional parts (red for halves, orange for thirds, yellow for fourths, green for sixths, blue for eighths and violet for twelfths).

●Abacus or counting frame. Children can make these by stringing colored beads on cords, the ends of which are run through holes in heavy cardboard or perforated hardboard. The cord is then drawn taut and knotted in back.

●Dominoes and/or pairs of dice for use in addition and subtraction practice.

●Sets of pictures can be used for a variety of purposes, from number concepts to word problems.

●Clock faces with movable hands.

●Decks (or parts of decks) of playing cards with face cards removed.

●Sets of three-dimensional objects such as small toys. Some of the many ways these may be used are to illustrate the concept of addition or subtraction, to make up or act out word problems, to show division or fractional parts of sets and to create sets and subsets.

●Envelopes of colored geometric shapes (cut from construction paper) for use in such activities as classifying by shape, measuring lengths of edges with a ruler, illustrating congruency, figuring area and perimeter, etc.

Pupil-Team Activities

Children frequently benefit from working in small groups of two, four or even five or six. Teams of two pupils can be used effectively for practice and extension work and problem solving activities in arithmetic, when the two partners are compatible and well-matched in ability and learning rate and style, with regard to the task involved in the activity. Teams containing four or five pupils can be given projects and planning, exploratory and other open-ended types of activities calling for divergent and expansive thinking. Pupil-team activities take advantage of the facts that children do learn from each other, that social interaction enhances task-oriented behavior and that cooperative effort toward a goal has its own built-in system of checks and balances.

In pupil-team activities, members of a team are encouraged to:

- discuss the assignment
- ask each other for help or explanations
- compare answers
- point out mistakes
- talk over problems
- share ideas
- evaluate their own and each other's work
- share the work
- read assignments aloud to each other
- discuss (debate) disagreements about the solution to or
- method of solving a problem
- share responsibility for the task
- compare work with answer keys when these are available.

An example of one way a two-man team situation can be used for the purpose of providing practice and extending skills in arithmetic is given in the team Assignment shown in Figure 9-3

Team Assignment
Problem Solving–Mixed Practice

I. Work with your partner to do this assignment. Decide which of you will be Partner "A" and which of you will be Partner "B". Use the price list below to help you solve the practice problems.

II. Practice problems.

1. "A" read problem aloud.   *Fresh Fruits and Vegetables*
"B" solve problem.

Corn	60¢ doz.
Tomatoes	29¢ basket
Beans	19¢ lb.
Squash	14¢ each
Apples	89¢ basket

"A" check "B's" answer.
Problem: If Mrs. Jones bought a dozen ears of corn and a basket of tomatoes, how much would her bill be?

2. "B" read problem aloud. "A" solve problem. "B" check "A's" answer. *Problem:* If Mrs. Jones owes 89¢, how much change will she get from a dollar?

III. Take turns reading, solving and checking the problems on p. 274, of your arithmetic book.

IV. Each partner make up and write three problems about the price list given above. Make one of them a hard problem. Trade papers and solve your partner's problems. Then return papers and check each other's work.

Figure 9-3

In this example, all parts of the assignment are related to solving word problems. Two practice problems are given to establish the working relationship pattern to be used with certain problems in the text. The last part of the assignment adds a little spice. Since children assigned to such teams have similar abilities regarding the skills, even the pupil-made "toughie" should be within the partner's range.

Individualized Independent Study

At times you will wish to have many of your students work independently on assignments you have given them or tasks of their own choosing. You may also find two or three children who will learn much more rapidly through independent study than through the slower process of teacher-led lessons. Also, a few children will prefer independent study to pupil-team activities and a few others will benefit more from it because their study habits do not promote good use of the pupil-team setting. Whatever specific purpose there may be for an independent study activity will influence the type of activity and its content. These will vary from pupil to pupil at a given time and from time to time for a given pupil.

Three examples of independent study activities are discussed briefly below. One of these activities was designed for a student who learns easily from printed material, who grasps arithmetic concepts and skills easily and who works well on his own. The second activity was planned for several students who had been involved in teacher-led lessons developing the skills of finding areas and perimeters of rectangles, and who were now ready for independent practice in these skills. The third activity described below was designed for pupils the teacher felt would benefit from reteaching and highly structured practice in addition with regrouping.

The activity planned for the able student who was a rapid and independent learner was in the nature of a long term, self-directing unit of study on other base systems. This project involved work with Base Five, Base Two and Base 12. The student was given a packet of materials which included the following items:

● A list of specific objectives.

● A resource chart giving page numbers (from three arithmetic texts) for (a) explanatory material, (b) self-correcting practice exercises and (c) exploratory or advanced activity options for each of the objectives of the unit.

● Evaluation activities with answer keys for self-testing for each objective.

• Checklists and progress charts for keeping track of his own progress and for communicating with the teacher at brief weekly conferences.

• Request forms for final teacher-administered evaluation of mastery for each objective.

As the student worked with the materials and objectives of the unit, he was able to pace himself according to the difficulty of the work and his own motivation. Weekly conferences were scheduled automatically and others could be held as requested by either the student or the teacher. Whenever the student felt ready to take a mastery test for one or more objectives he would notify the teacher by means of a request form.

Only with an occasional student will extended independent study such as this prove effective. A greater number, but still relatively few students, will be able to handle shorter term activities similar to this, perhaps dealing with a carefully selected single objective and lasting for a week or so. Some students may never be ready to work this way during the time they are with you.

Six students ready for individual practice in finding area and perimeter for rectangles were given a different type of independent activity. This study activity was designed for a one-week period. Provisions were made for differences in rate and for some degree of self-selection. Since this was considered a learning rather than a testing activity, answer keys were provided and student-kept progress records were in the form of simple bar graphs.

A set of 12 Area and Perimeter Practice Cards were made, each containing ten different, but equally difficult problems in area and perimeter. Six copies of a sample card were used for a small-group training session in which students became familiar with the format of the cards, ground rules for study periods and the methods for record keeping. The remainder of the first day's arithmetic time block plus those for the rest of the week were given over to independent pursuit of the activity. A minimum of six cards, and a maximum of ten was assigned, with each child free to select any of the cards and in any order. After the week's independent study, each of the six students was given one of the cards which he had not used. This card, without the accompanying answer key, was used for evaluation by the teacher. An example of one of these cards may be found in Figure 9-4.

The third independent study activity under discussion was planned as a reteaching and structured practice activity for use with children needing this type of review work in addition. The activity was designed as three tape-recorded practice sessions so that it could

Practice Card
Area and Perimeter

1. Find the area, in square inches, of the teacher's desk top.

2. What is the perimeter of our classroom floor?

3. My yard is 96 ft. wide and 168 ft. deep. My driveway is 24 ft. wide. I want to put a fence all around my yard except across the driveway. If fencing costs $35 per 8-foot length, how much will it cost me?

4. How many 1-foot square tiles will be needed to cover the ceiling of a room 24 feet by 36 feet?

5. What is the area of the house whose measurements are shown at the right?

   56' × *28'*

6. How many feet of gutter pipe will be needed to go around the perimeter of the roof of the house shown above if the roof hangs 1 foot farther out than the wall on each side?

7. Mrs. Quigley is making a patchwork quilt. She wants the quilt to be 72 inches wide and 120 inches long. How many 1-*foot* square patches will she need to make the quilt?

8. How many *feet* of edging will Mrs. Quigley need to go around the perimeter of her quilt?

9. Mr. and Mrs. Adams want to buy new carpeting for their living room. If their room is 15 ft. wide and 21 ft. long, how many square *yards* of carpeting will they need?

10. How much cheaper would it be for Mr. and Mrs. Adams to buy 1-foot square self-stick carpet tiles at $1.29 each for their room than to buy regular carpeting at $13.95 a square yard for it?

Figure 9-4

be used as needed. The taped directions called for manipulation of concrete materials as well as paper-and-pencil exercises. Step-by-step guidance was given for working through examples of addition with regrouping. In using this activity, a child was given one of the taped practice sessions and the necessary manipulative and worksheet materials. He was encouraged to go over the lesson as many times as he wanted to.

Immediate and delayed learning was tested by means of two follow-up paper-and-pencil worksheets. One of these was given immediately after the practice session and the other a few days later. The two other taped lessons could be used then, or later, with students still needing review and practice. If after three separate lessons with the taped sessions, a child still needed work in this area, further diagnosis and teacher-led activities based on the results of the diagnosis were introduced.

ACTIVITY- AND INTEREST-CENTERED APPROACHES

One of the basic assumptions underlying this book's approach to individualizing instruction is the need for providing many opportunities for meaningful self-selection of learning experiences and exploratory inquiry through the use of manipulative materials in the classroom setting. Child-oriented opportunities of these kinds relating directly or indirectly to the area of arithmetic can be provided in a number of ways. Two possible approaches will be discussed here—the establishment of a Math Interest Center and the introduction of a Math Activity Day into the regular instructional program. Both of these opportunities for self-selection and inquiry can also be adapted for use in other subject areas, as discussions in other chapters suggest.

Math Interest Center

A number of terms can be employed to describe the characteristics of an interest center: variety, action-oriented, availability, self-directing, intriguing, opportunity, exploratory, cooperation, options—to name a few. Let us consider each of these terms in relation to interest centers in general, keeping in mind that a *math* interest center will be unique only in terms of the content of activities.

Variety—An interest center will contain many different activities which cover a wide range of levels of difficulty, appeal to varied interests and learning styles and incorporate diverse formats and materials.

Action-Oriented—Most activities at an interest center will call for physical action and/or manipulation with a minimum of paper-and-pencil type materials.

Availability—Children will find it easy to locate, handle and use the materials and supplies at an interest center. Storage space and space for pursuing activities are child-oriented.

Self-Directing—Materials and activities at an interest center are either inherently self-explanatory or include easy-to-read-and-follow instructions. Some game formats may require introductory training. In many cases a few children can be taught how to play the game, and they, in turn, teach others.

Intriguing—Every attempt should be made to make interest center materials attractive, colorful and provocative. A really exciting and worthwhile activity is of no value if it isn't interesting looking enough to cause children to choose it.

Opportunity—Each child should have adequate time and freedom for using an interest center. If the activities are available only "when your other work is finished," many children will be severely limited in opportunity to use the center—often those who need it most.

Exploratory—Many activities at an interest center will be of an open-ended nature allowing for experimentation rather than calling for convergent thinking. (Where specific responses are required, some method of self-correction should be provided.)

Cooperation—Many activities at an interest center are designed for use by more than one student at a time. Games, many manipulative materials and experimental activities are some of the kinds of opportunities for cooperative effort which are included at an interest center.

Options—Since alternatives from which to choose and true freedom of choice are both requisite to meaningful self-selection, both are characteristic of interest center usage. Specific assignments or restrictions such as "don't use the same activity more than twice a week" or "select one activity from each category (or box or table) before choosing a second activity from any one category" are not part of the open option interest center.

The following suggestions for interest center activities are all math-oriented. The list is by no means exhaustive but contains examples of a variety of types of activities and formats for materials. Many formats adapt easily to other subject content.

Manipulative, Exploratory Materials

1. Equal arm balance, grocer's scale, bathroom scale
2. Compasses, protractors, T-square, triangles
3. Stop-watch, sweep second hand watch, kitchen timer
4. Assorted containers for liquid measure; dry measure
5. Tape measure, 6-ft. rule, yardstick, etc.
6. Geometric-shape building kits
7. Abacus, counting frame, assorted counting devices
8. Pegboard, pegs, yarn or rubber bands
9. Plumb line, carpenter's level, line level, transit
10. Manipulatives listed in section on teacher-led sessions.

Game Activities

1. Multiplication Casino—two players use a deck of playing cards from which jokers and face cards have been removed. Deal five cards to each player and ten cards face up on table. Players take turns as follows: using any one card from hand and any one from table, form a pair of numbers. To take the

trick, the player must name the product obtained when the two numbers are multiplied. If he cannot name the product correctly, he must leave the pair face up on the table. The tens of all four suits are wild cards and player assigns a value to the card before making a pair. When both players have used all cards and only unclaimed pairs remain on table, deal remaining cards, five to each player and ten face up on board. Play continues as before until only unclaimed pairs remain on table. Players take turns to claim tricks of unclaimed pairs by naming products. Game is over when all tricks are claimed or until no one can take remaining tricks. To score: nines are 3 points each; sevens and eights, 2 points each; sixes, 1 point each; the four of diamonds, 2 points; the two of spades, 1 point and all others no points. Greatest number of points wins.

2. Number Fact Checkers—Number the squares on a checkerboard and the checkers as shown in Figure 9-5.

Number Fact Checkers

9		8		9		8
	6		7		6		7
5		4		5		4	
	2		3		2		3
3		2		3		2	
	4		5		4		5
7		6		7		6	
	8		9		8		9

Figure 9-5

Before game starts, establish the appropriate operation—addition, subtraction or multiplication—for the game. Play proceeds as for regular checkers, except that the player must give correct number fact for each move. Thus if an 8 checker is moved to a 4 space and the game operation is addition, the player must call 12 before he may move his checker to the desired space. A wrong answer means player loses his turn. Players may arrange their checkers in any desired number pattern when setting up the board to start a game. When a player must king his opponent's man, he may choose any numbered checker and place it on top of the man being kinged. The top number is the one to use in figuring the number facts for subsequent moves.

Drill, Practice and Self-Testing Materials

1. Cross number puzzles
2. Math wheels
3. Bingo and lotto-type games
4. Flash cards
5. Mental arithmetic tapes
6. Number fact records
7. Puzzles, brainteasers and arithmetricks
8. Programmed arithmetic books
9. Math-in-acetate (worksheets and answer keys)

Activity Day

A second way to provide opportunities for self-selection and manipulative exploration is to introduce an Activity Day into the arithmetic program. One day each week is designated as Math Activity Day and the regular arithmetic time is devoted to short or long term projects chosen by each child.

Project options are designed to include a practical application of some type of arithmetic skill. A list of suggested activities is given to each child and one is posted on a bulletin board. Work areas, necessary equipment and some of the basic materials should be provided, but children can be expected to supply specialized materials required for the projects of their choice. One teacher installed in his classroom a workbench with woodworking tools and a "kitchen," which included a hot plate, portable oven, picnic ice chest and the classroom sink.

Several specific suggestions for four of the many possible types of activities are listed below. Many of these projects are adaptable for younger children.

Building Projects

1. Custom-designed dog house
2. Bird house or feeding station
3. Tie rack
4. Cutting board or cheese board
5. Doll house
6. Book ends
7. Toy chest
8. Bookcase

Kitchen Projects—Snacks for Entire Class

1. Chocolate Chip or oatmeal and raisin cookies
2. Fudge
3. Pudding
4. Popcorn and punch
5. Spiced tea
6. Gelatin salad
7. Ginger bread
8. Cheese ball and crackers

Models

1. Your bedroom
2. Scale model of the classroom (for experimenting with new arrangements)
3. Football field with players (to show defensive and offensive plays)
4. Doll size furniture (cardboard or wood)
5. Dioramas of any desired scene
6. Cars, boats, planes (made from scratch)
7. Blueprints, map of school yard, etc.
8. Supermarket, gas station, department store

Graphing Projects

1. Local temperatures (daily highs and lows for past week—data from newspapers)
2. Various weather data
3. Ball throwing records
4. Times required to complete various puzzles
5. Heights of children in class
6. Jump rope records
7. Data on favorite colors of classmates
8. Weights of various objects in classroom

Consider briefly the amount of applied arithmetic in just one of these projects—baking gingerbread, for example. In order to make enough for the entire class, a regular recipe will need to be doubled or trebled, including any fractional measurements. A decision will need to be made about the number and sizes of baking pans needed to accommodate the larger amount and the appropriate adjustments in baking time if needed. Actual measuring of ingredients, clock watching and oven temperature settings, all are measurement activities. Beating will involve either counting or timing. Division of the finished product into equivalent size servings will also be involved. Analysis of any of the projects will reveal multiple opportunities to apply arithmetic skills.

Summary

Commercially published arithmetic programs, which tend to be designed primarily on the basis of the logic of the discipline, can be modified in various ways so as to tailor them to a more child-centered approach.

The scope of a program can be adjusted to fit the rate of the majority of children in a classroom. It can be categorized into priority classifications for use in a three-group plan of instruction. Or the topics can be arranged in a single priority sequence for use in organizing a more highly individualized, continuous progress approach to instruction. Identifying logical options for altering the sequence of an arithmetic program also increases its flexibility and increases your opportunities to reorient the program according to certain child needs and interests.

An evaluation of specific children's styles and rates of learning arithmetic assists in identifying modifications in instructional techniques which can make the program more highly child-oriented. Such an evaluation provides a framework for selecting an appropriate balance among teacher-led, pupil-team and independent study activities for various children.

Child-oriented modifications which permit self-selection and exploratory inquiry can be provided through activity and interest-centered approaches. Math interest centers containing a wide variety of provocative activities and materials encourage exploration of many arithmetic concepts and skills. A once-a-week Math Activity Day can serve as a vehicle for providing many opportunities to apply arithmetic concepts and skills in practical, yet enjoyable projects.

Variation and Flexibility in Science

10

In most classrooms today science is taught by one of three methods: the textbook, the action-oriented program, or the ignore-it-and-maybe-it-will-go-away approach. The textbook method generally emphasizes the acquisition of information such as definitions of terms, explanations of processes and relationships and descriptions and examples of various classifications of things—mammals, sedimentary rocks and planets, for example. Several action-oriented programs available today stress the child's involvement in various components of the scientific process, including such activities as measuring, recording data, hypothesizing, observing, planning controlled experiments and drawing conclusions from empirical data. The ignore-it-and-maybe-it-will-go-away approach may occasionally be stretched just enough to permit a classroom display of science library books and a "science corner" with a goldfish bowl and a box of magnets. The ignore-it approach is often employed by teachers who are afraid of teaching science, who think they don't know enough about it or who say they can't find time in the school day to teach it. Actually the science books, the goldfish bowl and the box of magnets could provide the beginning of an exciting science program for the teacher who doesn't mind if the children learn about science as long as she doesn't have to teach it to them.

Differentiated instruction in science, by whatever method you choose to employ, will benefit from an underlying unity of purpose. A functional understanding of the scientific method is a desirable overall goal for the science program, and as such provides the necessary unity in direction and purpose. Attitudes and skills used in the scientific method of investigation can be learned and applied with an unlimited variety of specific contexts and within the structure of any instructional strategy. Students should become involved in stating problems in a suitable form for guiding investigation. They should learn to speculate on the probable outcome of an investigation (form an hypothesis). And, they should actively take part in testing their hypotheses, analyzing results and carrying out any subsequent explorations that may become necessary to the satisfactory solution of their stated problems.

Whichever type of science program you employ in your classroom: textbook, process approach or ignore-it, and whatever specific topics, units and content you include, you will find in this chapter many suggestions to help you bring variation and flexibility to your program.

A FRAMEWORK FOR LONG RANGE ACTIVITIES

Many science activities require long periods of time for completion. In some cases, the need for frequent repetitions of an activity throughout the year may be the reason for long range planning. In other situations, the need for year-long involvement may stem from the desirability of providing many sequential variations of a given activity or from the extensive time required to wait for results of certain activities. Whatever the reasons may be, you will find it worthwhile to provide both a physical organization in your classroom and a curricular organization in your planning which will accommodate long term involvement in science-related activities.

Lab Centers and Science Stations

Physical provisions for long-range science activities can include the establishment of lab centers and science stations. These centers and stations may be rather general and flexible in nature or they may be designed for a rather specific purpose. Examples of each are included in the suggestions given below.

The Wet Lab Center

Every classroom should have some sort of wet lab center where activities requiring water and other liquids can be carried out. It should, rather obviously, be near the sink if you have one, and if you do not have one the wet lab should provide pails for clean water and for waste liquids. Water can be obtained and waste liquids disposed of in the custodian's area or in lavatories in most schools. A second essential characteristic for a wet lab center is easy cleaning up. Plenty of sponges, cloths and paper towels, a mop, broom and dust pan and large trash containers are minimum requirements. Linoleum or oilcloth covering the floor in the wet lab area will give added protection. The use of plastic or metal containers whenever possible will cut down on glass breakage which is dangerous and expensive as well as messy. Adequate storage space for supplies and in-process projects makes the center more efficient as well as more attractive. Of course, a center such as this can be used for short term as well as long term projects, but the center itself should be a year-long installation.

Action Research Center

An action research center can be an extended variation of a wet lab. Essentially it is a fairly large area established for the purpose of conducting science experiments. The area may be subdivided into a Biology Station, a Physics and Chemistry Station, an Earth Science Station, etc. Such divisions are largely a matter of the label given a specific space and the type of supplies and projects stored there. Some substations in an action research center may be maintained year long, while others may change their labels and characteristic activities from time to time throughout the year. For example, the Earth Science Station may subsequently become a Space Station or a Prehistory Station while the Biology Station remains as is all year.

Portable Weather Station

A portable weather station is an intriguing addition to the classroom's science equipment. Designs of various degrees of sophistication can be devised to meet your specific requirements. Children will enjoy the challenge of designing and building such a weather station. Two suggestions are given here to illustrate first a very simple and then a more complex version of a portable weather station.

The simplest design calls for a small wooden box with a hinged door (or lid) which can be fastened while the box is being carried. A thermometer should be screwed to one inside wall of the box in such a way that, when the box is set in an open, sunny spot, the thermometer will be shaded from the direct sun and yet will be easy to read. Compartments in the box can be built to safely and securely hold other instruments such as a barometer and a compass. An old spice cabinet with padding in the drawers may serve for this purpose. A clipboard or envelope for holding data records may be fastened to the inside of the door or may be kept in a special compartment in the box. A telescoping antenna from an old radio or television set may be fastened to the outside of the box. A pennant type flag stored in the box when not in use may be fastened to the extended antenna to serve as a wind vane. Used in conjunction with the compass, the wind vane will indicate wind direction. See Figure 10-1. This version of the portable weather station may be carried outside whenever desired. Adequate time should be allowed to permit the thermometer to register accurately the outside temperature.

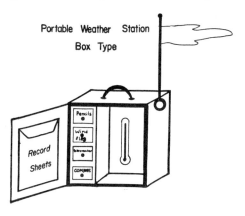

Figure 10-1

A second version of the portable weather station is designed to be left outdoors for the entire school day, or longer, if desired. It is built around the central pole of a discarded umbrella-type clothes drying pole. A pipe driven into the ground to receive the pole may be placed in an open yard or field preferably within sight and easy reach of the classroom. Weather instruments may be mounted and appropriately sheltered or exposed according to their specific purposes. A telescoping antenna may again be used to raise a more sophisticated wind sock to the highest possible elevation. A waterproof container for data recording tables, instructions for using and reading instruments, illustrated charts of cloud types and formations, etc. should be easily accessible. A writing shelf would be highly desirable. Get some of your students busy designing and building this type of portable weather station to meet your class's specific requirements.

Information Retrieval Station

An information retrieval station can be devoted entirely to science or it may be shared with other subject areas. It is essentially a place for library type research and should contain the following sources of information:

- Science textbooks, trade books, paperbacks, encyclopedias, dictionaries, atlases, almanacs ...

- Magazines, science bulletins, newspapers, booklets, leaflets, U.S. government science-related publications, student-prepared reports ...
- Filmstrips, filmloops, slides, tapes, records, transparencies ... and the necessary A-V equipment
- A bulletin board or part of one devoted to Science in the News
- Space for science-related displays or exhibits made by students or the teacher or obtained from museums and libraries
- A student-designed filing system and card catalog
- Student-compiled bibliographies (always growing) on popular topics
- A vertical file of pictures, charts, graphs, newspaper clippings and magazine articles

Centers for Younger Pupils

The types of lab centers and science stations described above may be more appropriate for middle and upper elementary and early secondary students. However, the concept of lab centers and science stations can easily be modified to meet the interests and abilities of younger pupils. Here are some examples you might wish to try.

1. *A Sorting and Classifying Station*—Provide lots of things to sort: stones, shells, assorted macaroni and pasta, dried peas and beans, pictures of flowers, pictures of animals, small toys, candy, food, etc. and lots of things to sort into: egg cartons, an old jewelry box, fisherman's tackle box, canister sets, post office type filing box, assorted cardboard boxes, envelopes, jars, paper cups, etc.

2. *A Gardening Table*—Provide a dishpan full of soil, assorted cans and plastic containers, spoons and forks to till the soil, assorted seeds, plant labels for names, dates and seed names, a soda pop can for a watering can and a window ledge with sunlight.

3. *A Collection Corner*—Provide a place for children to display their collections and to house class collections in the process of growing.

4. *A Measuring Center*—Provide all sorts of thing to measure and weigh and the equipment or containers with which to measure and weigh them. Try to provide for a variety of types of measuring activities—dry, liquid, avoirdupois, linear, time, speed, temperature, etc.

5. *An Animal World*—Provide a featured animal each month for the children to observe and care for: an insect cage, white mice,

guinea pigs, an ant farm, gerbils, a rabbit, a baby chick, a puppy, kittens, tropical fish, a terrarium with salamanders, turtles, a parakeet or canary, hamsters, etc. Your local humane society may be able to provide you with animals and cages on loan, together with information on the care and feeding of various animals.

A Problem Centered Approach to Differentiation in Science

Curricular organization can also be planned to provide for long term or ongoing activities. Given a specific situation or set of circumstances, and triggering experimental explorations by means of carefully worded questions, you can maintain a high level of interest and activity over a long period of time. Examples using such relevant and popular focal points as gerbils, ecology, gardening and weather will serve as illustrations.

Gerbil City Laboratories

Gerbils are inexpensive, easily obtained, easy to care for and fun. Teachers do not always take advantage of the vast potential gerbils offer for science activities. They can serve as a basis for year long research both in the library and in the classroom "laboratory." Try to obtain four gerbils. Start the year by having your students design and build a city for the gerbils. The design of the city and its subsequent laboratory and the types of observations and experimenting to be undertaken are all guided and initiated by questions posed on problem cards. Questions such as the following are introduced at appropriate times, throughout the year:

●What activities do gerbils *require* which we *must* provide for them in Gerbil City?

●What activities do gerbils enjoy which we may provide for them if we wish?

●What is the proper method and menu for feeding gerbils?

●What kind of exercise do gerbils need and how can we design a gymnasium and recreational park for them?

●Do gerbils prefer to be together or do they like to be alone most of the time?

●In what ways are all our gerbils alike? In what ways are some of them different from the others?

●How would you describe the "personality" of each of our gerbils?

●Do all of our gerbils seem to want or need the same amount of food, sleep, exercise, chewing?

●How would you describe the eating habits of each one?

●Do our gerbils exhibit different eating habits when food is always available than when they are fed only at specified times and only for specified lengths of time?

●Can gerbils be trained to tell the difference between a black door and a white door? (The design of this experiment may require considerable use of guiding questions.)

●How do gerbils behave when they are kept in separate "homes" and not allowed to visit and play together?

●Which gerbil is the champion racer; cardboard tube chewer; maze runner; highest climber; longest treadmill runner?

Classroom Farming

The recent popularity of home vegetable gardening makes this a timely as well as a perpetually interesting focal topic for students. The idea of indoor vegetable and fruit raising is relatively novel, and its practical potential gives added intrigue to classroom experimentation along this line. Seed companies are producing varieties of some vegetables especially for flower pot and windowsill gardening. Miniature varieties requiring small space and producing tennis ball-size lettuce and cabbage heads, small carrots, cucumbers, tomatoes, etc. offer a wide range of possibilities for indoor experimentation. Questions posed on problem cards can guide experimentation with artificial lights, sun lamps, fertilizers, humidity control, etc. Correspondence with the seed companies and agricultural colleges might yield valuable suggestions and information.

In warmer regions of the country outdoor gardening could be a worthwhile focus of experimental activity. Even in some of the cooler areas, short term or early-bearing vegetables and fruits might be considered. Radishes, green peas, snap beans, leaf lettuce, Swiss chard and beet greens are a few possibilities. Perennials such as strawberries, rhubarb and asparagus are early harvest crops but do not generally yield until the second year. Some miniature fruit trees can be grown and brought into production indoors, but again this is a long term project. Such "crops" might be undertaken as an ongoing total school activity. A few schools have or might consider adding a greenhouse. A classroom teacher who is really enthused could consider a makeshift class-built greenhouse of some sort.

Research Teams

Four-man teams of students interested in some specific type of science-related projects can engage in a diversified program of activities under the unifying classification of research teams. One such team interested in pollution prevention and control can work cooperatively with community action groups and/or other student groups from the same school. They may become the class's Pollution Control Squad. Another group involved in weather data gathering, reporting and predicting might use a portable weather station such as described earlier as a base of operations. The Weather Researchers could engage in a long term search for patterns of change in weather indicators which they feel can be used as predictors for weather forecasting. Another group, perhaps electing to call themselves Stargazers, might be involved in a study of star movements, the solar system, comets, eclipses and other phenomena of outer space. Birdwatchers, Rockhounds, Electricians and Chemists are other possibilities for student teams "researching" in varied ways their diverse areas of interest.

A Journal of Scientific Research

Any type of experimental endeavor and many types of library research on scientific topics can be "written up" and "published" in a class Journal of Scientific Research. A paper written for the Journal should include a statement of the hypothesis, problem or question under investigation. A description of the experimental method employed or a resume of library research read should also be included in the report. The paper should conclude with a discussion of the findings and the researcher's reaction to the findings and the study in general.

A device such as this type of Journal serves as much more than a purpose for writing a report. The task helps the student organize his data, it requires that he think about the implications of his findings and may assist him in planning future investigations. Writing these "scientific papers" is also a beginning introduction to the role and use of research journals as used in many discipline areas.

OPPORTUNITIES FOR DIVERSE SHORT TERM PROJECTS

Many teachers find that it is easier to arrange for diversity and flexibility in the science program by providing options and differentiated opportunities in short term projects than when organizing for year long activities. Short blocks of time devoted to diversification of science projects can be alternated with periods of more traditional large group activities. An organizational plan which alternates between textbook-oriented or teacher-led lessons and independently selected and performed student activities is a good way to move into differentiation in the science program. Such a plan permits the teacher as well as the students to sample the less structured approach in small doses followed by periods of more familiar (and perhaps more comfortable by virtue of this familiarity) whole class, teacher-directed sessions. The familiar format of the latter periods offers everyone an opportunity to reconnoiter the new strategies, assess problems and reactions and plan the next foray into new instructional territories without a feeling of being hurdled along on an uncontrollable wave of confusion. Teachers new to the concept of self-selection and multidirectional activity will do well to start slowly and pause frequently for reassessment and new planning.

Focusing-in on Student Specialties

One of the easiest and least involved ways to offer options for self-selection is to capitalize on existing interests and hobbies. Almost every student has some specialty or area of special interest, and frequently these are science related. You can provide many kinds of opportunities for student sharing of these specialties.

1. Brainstorming sessions where children in groups of four or five think of as many examples as they can of

- Plant-related objects to collect
- Animal-related objects to collect
- Nonplant and nonanimal objects to collect
- Kinds of insects to collect for observation in an insect cage
- Things that can be made to operate with dry cell batteries
- Things to do with pulleys . . . magnets . . . wind . . .
- Words about reptiles . . . the universe . . . plants . . .
- Things to look for in the woods

2. Small group share-and-tell about science-related things the children have done or seen

- Visits to exhibits and museums
- Trips to see natural wonders
- Tours of factories, electrical plants, dams
- Field Trips taken in past
- Television shows
- Visits to planetariums, greenhouses or conservatories
- Trips to zoos, aquariums, humane societies, fish hatcheries, game preserves
- Interesting science books, articles or news items seen recently.

3. One-at-a-time hobby show—instead of having a large scale, all-at-once hobby exhibit, have only one or two children bring in their science hobbies each day to share with others. Provide them with time to explain and/or demonstrate their chemistry set, plastic

prehistoric animal collection, microscope, self-built electrical device, album of bird pictures, tropical fish, set of science books, unknown animal skull, jar of insects or box of stones. Provide opportunity for nonparticipation or passive participation for those students who feel they have nothing to share or who wish merely to bring in for display but do not want to talk about their contributions.

4. Special interest groups or clubs can be formed for short term projects. Individuals or small groups of students should select a topic of special interest to them and prepare visual projects to illustrate some aspect of their topics. Be prepared to offer varied suggestions for those students who are not able to identify a topic. Often your suggestions will stimulate their own ideas but a few may select from the offered topics one which appeals to them. Here are 30 suggestions to start your list.

- Dinosaurs
- What makes color?
- Sulfuric acid
- The four seasons
- Precious gems
- Weeds you can eat
- Atoms and atomic force
- What happens to frogs in winter?
- A plant's life: From seed to seed
- Poisons
- How water gets up a tree
- How some animals "sleep" all winter
- The ocean bottom
- Beyond the solar system
- Light, lenses and prisms
- How do you know that air is there?
- How does a compass work?
- How does a snake move?
- A few ways to make electricity
- What is water?
- Plants that eat animals
- What makes a motorcycle go?
- The most unusual animal I know
- Wanted: Clean air
- Why does an onion make you cry?
- Microscopic wonders
- Wheels do marvelous things
- What makes the sound of music?

● What shall we do with all our garbage?
● How do animals talk?

5. Student-taught lessons offer interesting opportunities to share for those students who have become somewhat expert in a particular aspect of science. Three fourth grade students with widely different personalities and interests volunteered to teach science lessons to their class. Due largely to each student's long-standing enthusiasm for his topic and the use of the student's equipment and paraphernalia for illustration and demonstration purposes, each lesson was both informative and interesting.

The first lesson was taught by a tiny girl who was a real bug on butterflies and moths. She brought in examples from her extensive collection and used them to explain differences between moths and butterflies. She discussed some local varieties of each, their habits and habitats and told how she caught her specimens. Using her own equipment, she explained how to use the nets, killing jar and mounting materials. She also discussed the many ways in which the local museum had been helpful to her in her hobby.

A very withdrawn and scholastically underachieving youngster taught the second lesson. His discussion centered around how he had made, from bits and scrap pieces, a two-way radio. He also described what made the two-way radio work and gave each child an opportunity to use it. Considerable information about the purpose and workings of many of the inner parts of the radio was forthcoming and several boys in the class embarked on electrical projects with this youngster as their engineer.

The third lesson was taught by a camera buff. Bringing in his own two cameras, his developing equipment and several mounted examples of his work, he used these objects as the focal points of his lesson. The first part was a description of the way a camera works when a picture is being taken, the second part was a discussion of the chemistry and process of black-and-white film development and the final aspect of the lesson was a talk about selecting nature study subjects for photographing. Following the lesson the "pupil teacher" used his Polaroid camera to take pictures of all children in the class in small group settings. These were mounted and displayed on the bulletin board as part of his week long photography exhibit.

Lessons taught by pupils do not usually come in complete, neat, sophisticated little packages. But what they lack in finesse they make up for in enthusiasm and relevance to children. Rarely have I known of a student-taught lesson which failed to generate a splurge of interested activity in at least a few other children in the class.

Instructional Units and Textbook Coverage

For the teacher who either feels obligated by administrative edict to utilize a syllabus or textbook as the science program or feels uncomfortable in venturing too far from the syllabus or textbook, there are ways in which even such a highly structured curriculum can achieve variation, flexibility and differentiation. The teacher who adopts an alternating structured and action-oriented approach may also find herself seeking ways to at least partially modify the structured portions of the program. Suggestions given below are designed specifically to be used with syllabus and textbook units although they may be adapted to other uses. The major emphasis here is to avoid page-by-page coverage and total reliance on whole class activities.

Job Sheets and Contracts

Job sheets and contracts, as the terms are used here, serve virtually the same purpose. They are designed to outline a series of tasks requiring more than one day which students will engage in at their own rates of speed and on an independent or small group basis.

A *job sheet* lists tasks and the instructions, materials or books needed and any required finished product for each task. Some provision should be made for the student to record his progress as he works his way through a job sheet. All children in a class may be given the same job sheet in which case self-pacing is the only real provision for differentiation. Or a teacher may elect to prepare two or more job sheets of varying degrees of difficulty covering basically the same concepts but providing additional differentiation to accommodate variations in reading level, performance skills, study habits and rate and styles of learning. Optional activities may also be included to offer some degree of self-selection.

A *contract* must contain some options for student choice. The options may take the form of alternative tasks listed on a given contract sheet or they may take the form of alternative contract sheets from which each student chooses the one or ones he wishes to pursue. In addition to provision for self-selection, a contract usually asks for some commitment on the part of the student—at least a statement that this is the activity the student has selected to do, and, if desired, an estimate of how long he expects the project will take him to complete.

Activities such as the three that follow may be among the tasks listed on job sheets or contracts. They may also be employed separately without any connection with either job sheets or contracts. All three activities are related to the same unit of study.

Study Guides

To guide a student in his independent or small team study of a textbook or other printed selection, a teacher may elect to utilize a study guide. Such a guide is designed to direct the student as he engages in a short-term information retrieval activity. The time required to complete the work involved in a study guide should not exceed that allowed for one (or possibly two) day's scheduled science period. An example of a study guide designed to accompany a part of a science textbook chapter on the topic Rocks and Minerals is shown in Figure 10-2.

Study Guide
Rocks and Minerals

I. Textbook pp. 78-79	Skim these pages to find the three major kinds of rocks. List them. Give two examples of each. 1. 2. 3.
II. Textbook pp. 80-82	Read and define the following terms: 1. Magma— 2. Lava— 3. Volcano— 4. Eruption—
III. Textbook p. 83	Study carefully the diagram and text. Draw a series (at least four) of illustrations showing the growth of a volcanic mountain from beginning to full growth. Label your drawings or write a description to tell what happens at the different stages of a volcanic mountain's growth.

Figure 10-2

Text-Related Science Station

A short-term science station focusing on the topic under study can be established for any syllabus or textbook unit. Student work at these stations can be assigned, optional or a combination of the two. Assignments can be made in several ways. As mentioned earlier, a job sheet or contract can include science station tasks. Specific tasks can be assigned to the total class or differing tasks can be specifically assigned to individuals or groups, perhaps for later sharing with the rest of the class. Option assignments can also be made, such as "do any one of the following" or "select and do any three activities at the science station." A science station related to a unit on Rocks and Minerals could contain the following features:

- A pile of assorted rocks to sort and classify
- Equipment for testing hardness, cleavage, etc.
- Mounted collection of sedimentary, igneous and metamorphic rocks
- Mounted collections of minerals, ores and semiprecious gems
- A sediment jar (large glass or clear plastic jar half filled with large pebbles, small pebbles and sand in water, which, when shaken and allowed to stand, will illustrate sedimentary layering)
- A museum-loaned diorama depicting a coal mine
- A take-apart-put-together model of a volcano cross section
- Magazines for clipping illustrations of ways in which rocks and minerals are used in our society
- Experiment cards guiding activities such as testing for limestone, classifying rock and mineral specimens, simulating sedimentary rock formation
- Filmstrips and other audio-visual materials on earthquakes, volcanoes, fossils, gems, erosion, mining, prehistoric land forms, theories regarding formation of Earth, the Earth's interior, limestone caves, etc.
- Books, charts, diagrams, etc. related to the unit
- Exhibit area for display of student projects and collections

Activity Cards

A variety of formats can be used in preparing sets of activity cards for use with any science unit being studied. Activity cards can be included as part of the science station paraphernalia or may constitute a separate type of assigned or unassigned task. Card activities should be either open-ended in nature or should include answer keys for self-correction whenever possible. Ten possible formats are described briefly below, with examples drawn from the Rocks and Minerals unit used as illustrations.

1. *Phrase Analysis*—On one side of a 5 x 8 card print a collection of terms or phrases such as cooled magma, volcanic mountain, limestone caves, basalt formation, conglomerate, etc. which the student is to list under two or three classifications (also printed on the front of the card—i.e., Sedimentary, Igneous). Cor-

rectly classified lists may be printed on the reverse side of the card for self-correction. Eight or more cards, each with different phrases to be analyzed would constitute a set. One set for each unit studied during the year would be a valuable addition to the classroom's supply of teacher-made materials.

2. *Mind-Benders*—Several sets of ten or more mind-bender cards would be worthwhile since a child can work through a set rather quickly. Each card has a tough or tricky question or a riddle on one side, and the answer on the back. Figure 10-3 gives examples of three mind-bender cards.

Mind-Bender Cards

Figure 10-3

3. *Cards to Sort*—Try to accumulate about 100 small pictures which relate to any aspect of the unit under study. Mount each picture on an oaktag card and cover with transparent adhesive vinyl. Children can use these cards to sort into a variety of classification

categories. Let the children establish their own systems of classification and keep a list of the different ways in which they have classified the pictures.

4. *Sequence Cards*—These are sets of four or more picture cards which can be arranged into order which show the steps in coal mining, formation of a volcano, development of a fossil, formation of a sedimentary rock canyon, "life" of a diamond, etc. Sentence or paragraph cards can also be used for arranging in sequence to describe any process relating to the topic under study.

5. *Matching*—Pairs of cards that match or go together in some way are used to make up this set of activity cards. Words, sentences, phrases, pictures and drawings can all be used for matching terms with definitions, labels with examples, related examples, processes with products, materials with uses, etc.

6. *Word Puzzle Activities*—Cards can be used to hold various kinds of science-related word puzzles. Scrambled words, mini-crossword puzzles and word hunts are examples. A set of word puzzle cards can be created for each science unit studied and carried over for use another year. Children working in four-man brainstorming teams for about five minutes can provide you with an adequate supply of words relating to any given topic they are familiar with. Supplement their lists with a few of your own and you will be in business.

7. *Dial-an-Answer*—A bit of advance preparation is required to produce these activity cards. An oaktag (or heavier) card about 9 x 12 inches plus a 5-inch circle cut from similar material and a brass paper fastner will be needed for each card. The activity requires a child to read a question, decide on an answer and dial a series of numbers, much as he would dial a lock combination, to check his answer with the correct one. Eight or 12 answer spaces fit conveniently around the dial wheel. A question box may contain a question for each answer given or some "dummy" answers may be inserted which are not correct responses for any of the questions. A simplified version of a Dial-an-Answer card is given in Figure 10-4.

8. *True-False Sort*—This is an easy activity to produce which children will enjoy making and adding to as well as using. Simply print a collection of true statements and false statements on 3 x 5 cards. Print only one statement on each card. The child sorts the cards into True and False piles. To correct, he turns cards over to check for a T or F on the back.

9. *Card Game*—To make this activity, prepare a set of 40 or more picture cards about the size of playing cards. Old playing cards

DIAL-AN-ANSWER

Question Box	
1. Islands formed by volcanoes are the _____. (Ans. 1, 4, 2)	2. Magma and lava always mean the same thing. True or False? (Ans. 3, 2, 3)
3. Marble is an example of _____. (Ans. 2, 5, 4)	4. An example of sedimentary rock formation is found at _____. (Ans. 4, 2, 3)

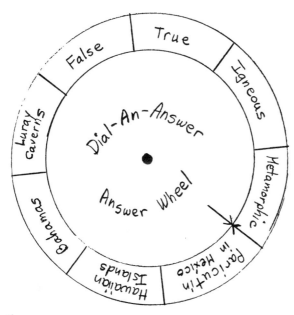

Instructions:

1. Line up the arrows.
2. Read a question, decide on correct answer.
3. To check answer, move arrow according to the numbers given for answer. For example, if numbers shown are 1, 4, 2, move arrow counterclockwise 1 space, clockwise 4 spaces and counterclockwise 2 spaces. Arrow will be pointing at correct response.

Figure 10-4

to which pictures have been pasted and covered with transparent adhesive vinyl may be used. Use rules similar to those used in playing *Authors*. Four related picture cards would form a book or set. Ten sets for use in connection with a Rocks and Minerals unit might include fossils, sedimentary rocks, igneous rocks, metamorphic rocks, gemstones, mineral ores, famous volcanoes, fuel minerals, Earth's layers and limestone cave formations. Words identifying the book classification and the name of the specific example should also be printed on the picture card.

10. *List 10*—This game is played with two or more people or teams. Several instruction cards are shuffled and placed face down on the table. One card is turned over and read aloud. An egg timer may be used if desired to identify a maximum time limit for each card. The first individual or team to list in writing ten legitimate examples of the category given on the card, or the team having the closest to ten correct responses when the time limit is up, scores 1 point. Greatest number of points at the end of the game wins. Cards may contain such category instructions as these.

- Things you might do if you found a stone you thought might be very valuable.
- Ways to use marble in a building
- Examples of minerals
- Things to do to identify an unknown rock specimen
- Examples of sedimentary (or igneous) rocks

EVALUATION AND THE DIFFERENTIATED PROGRAM

The differentiated science program, like all other aspects of differentiated or individualized instruction, demands unique consideration in solving problems of evaluation and accountability. Where goals and objectives, content and method, scope and sequence differ from child to child, evaluation must also differ. Process-oriented approaches cannot be measured by the same devices as are used to evaluate content-oriented programs. Objectives dealing with information acquisition and concept formation require evaluative techniques which vary from those used to measure "thinking skills" or objectives reaching into the affective domain. A teacher whose program goes beyond unilateral, preconceived goals, content and instruction should receive the courtesy of differentiated and individualized evaluation of her program in the accountability encounter.

Evaluation of student progress and of the teacher's effectiveness must go beyond a simple use of standardized achievement test scores if it is to be meaningful and relevant to the differentiated program.

This is not to say that standardized achievement testing does not have a role here; it is merely to suggest that evaluation should not be limited to grade level norms and percentile scores obtained on paper-and-pencil test instruments which measure a relatively narrow range of objectives.

Evaluation of student progress in the differentiated science program is many-faceted. It should be an ongoing not merely an end-of-year or end-of-semester activity. Perhaps the most valuable tool a teacher can have for this purpose is an ability to clearly state the objectives in question. Many science-related objectives lend themselves to nice, neat evaluative measuring. For example, the objective which expects the student to be able to "define and give examples of the following terms . . ." can easily be measured. An objective requiring that the student be able to "measure and record measurements according to the following criteria of accuracy:"

A Fahrenheit thermometer to within 2°
An aneroid barometer to within .1"
A volume of liquid to within ¼ oz. etc.

can also be evaluated with relative ease.

Objectives such as one to the effect that the student will employ the scientific method in dealing with questions posed to him are not as simple to evaluate nor do they lend themselves readily to paper-and-pencil tests or easily observable activity test situations. When objectives reach the affective domain of "feelings" and "attitudes," measurement becomes even more difficult and subjective. The idea that an objective stating that a student will *enjoy* science-related activities can be reduced to items such as "will voluntarily select science-related activities during free time" seems a bit stilted and artificial. Perhaps we would do as well to admit that some goals are virtually impossible to measure in a strictly objective way and then learn to live with the less tangible, more subjective aspects of evaluation.

Once objectives have been stated, and realizing that they will vary among students in a given class, relevant evaluation can be designed. Whenever possible, tangible, objective evaluation is preferred. When not appropriate, the best possible subjective measurement is better than no measurement or irrelevant measurement. Some formal or informal means of criterion reference testing can be used for many objectives in a differentiated science program. Whenever it fits in with what you are trying to do and whenever it stands up to the test of critical scrutiny, by all means use commercially available testing devices. Such a practice will save you work and can serve as a valuable evaluative tool if you are aware of both the strengths and the limitations of the instruments being used. Do not be afraid to devise your own evaluative techniques when you feel it is necessary, but always be careful to use your objectives as a frame of reference when designing these techniques and instruments. Keep in mind the value of diagnosis and of pre- and posttesting as an integral part of your program. Coupled with adequate and careful record keeping, these formal and informal means of testing will provide you with an evaluation program which has a broader base than that of standardized achievement tests alone.

Summary

Both the content-oriented science program and the process-centered approach require variation and flexibility to allow for differentiation of instruction and student involvement. A physical organization which provides a flexible framework for long range activities includes lab centers and science stations. Curricular organization can also enhance variation and flexibility as illustrated by examples of a problem-centered approach. Provision for diversity in short term activities is equally important to the science program and is perhaps easier to achieve through such techniques as taking advantage of unique student interests and projects. Introducing variety and options for self-selection into the textbook or syllabus-centered program turns the focus away from whole class lessons and page-by-page textbook coverage through the use of self-directing and independent activities.

A teacher involved with a content-oriented program can provide for greater individualization and self-direction through adaptation of such suggestions as the action research center, a sorting and classifying station, gerbil city laboratories and activity cards. The process-centered approach may be broadened and enhanced by utilizing suggestions regarding the retrieval of information, syllabus and textbook coverage and student specialties. A teacher employing an ignore-it-and-maybe-it-will-go-away science program will find it both rewarding and comfortable to explore such possibilities as the wet lab center, information retrieval center, a gardening table, student taught lessons or phrase analysis cards.

Evaluation and accountability in the differentiated instructional program goes beyond consideration of grade level norms and percentile ratings. While such scores, resulting from the administration of standardized achievement tests, can contribute to evaluation, they cannot be considered to comprise the whole of it. To be comprehensive and meaningful, evaluation and accountability programs must take into consideration measurement of a wide variety of kinds of objectives which are not likely to be identical for many students.

Index

205